Overcoming
Underearning™

Overcoming Underearning™

A Five-Step Plan to a Richer Life

Barbara Stanny

HARPER

NEW YORK · LONDON · TORONTO · SYDNEY

HARPER

HarperCollins books may be purchased for educational, business,
or sales promotional use. For information, please e-mail the
Special Markets Department at SPsales@harpercollins.com.

First Collins paperback edition published 2007

Designed by Ellen Cipriano

Library of Congress has catalogued the hardcover edition as follows:

Library of Congress Cataloging-in-Publication Data

Stanny, Barbara.
Overcoming underearning : overcome your money fears and earn what you deserve /
by Barbara Stanny.
p. cm.
Includes index.
ISBN-13: 978-0-06-081861-6
ISBN-10: 0-06-081861-1
1. Finance, Personal—Handbooks, manuals, etc. 2. Income—United States. I. Title.

HG179.S7947 2005
332.024'01—dc22 2005051939

ISBN-13: 978-0-06-081862-3 (pbk.)

19 20 CG/LSC 20 19 18 17 16 15

"All the music I write is a search for myself."

—Bruce Hornsby

Contents

SECTION 3: ENSURING SUCCESS

APPENDIX

Index

Acknowledgments

My heart overflows with gratitude for all the True Believers who've made *Overcoming Underearning*™ possible. This book was conceived in the wake of a very difficult period in my life. A series of crises, including my father's unexpected death, had me questioning my purpose, wondering what to do, unsure if I even wanted to continue writing. I felt lost, confused, frustrated.

One night, a few months after my father died, I had a dream. My father came to me and said, "I know what you're supposed to do next." I felt such joy when he told me, but as soon as I woke up, I forgot what he said, which left me even more frustrated. Less than a week later, however, everything fell into place.

That's when my fabulous editor, Leah Spiro, called. I'd given her the workbook from my Overcoming Underearning™ workshops some time ago. We talked about turning it into a book, but nothing happened. Suddenly, out of the blue, she says, "I think we should get started on it now."

Leah, I can't begin to thank you enough for your encouragement and unwavering support. Working with you has not only been supremely rewarding, both personally and professionally, but your belief in this project got me back in my groove.

I am bowled over by the whole team at HarperCollins: Joseph Tessitore, Larry Hughes, Marion Maneker, Libby Jordan, Tony Valado, Tara Cibelli, and Maggie Sivon. What a privilege to work with such an amazing group. And to Steve Hanselman, your confidence in me from the beginning is something I will always treasure.

The same goes for my awesome agent, Candice Fuhrman. You've gone to bat for me with every book, but you've gone that extra mile with this one. You're the best, Candice. Thank you doesn't quite cover it.

Oriana Green, you appeared like an angel during that difficult year. I hired you as my assistant. But you quickly became so much more: my Internet guru, marketing coordinator, video producer, speaking coach, book editor, and close friend. But above all, you became my mentor. You pushed me into my Discomfort Zone more times than I can count, and no matter how hard I kicked and screamed, you would never let me off the hook. My gratitude goes deeper than you know.

I also thank my dear friend, Marcia Brixey. The workshops would never have grown as they did without your tireless marketing skills. Plus you challenged me to think bigger, and then pushed me to go the distance. Together, we changed more lives than I could ever have done alone. And we had a lot of fun doing it.

To Barbara Lombardo, and all the talented folks at Monteiro and Company, how blessed I am to have found you. You're the best publicist an author could ever wish for. I adore working with you.

Karen McCall, my heartfelt thanks for your patient coaching, your genuine compassion, and the pioneering work you've done in this field. I don't know where I'd be without your support! I count you among my closest friends.

Again, Doris Ober, your feedback made all the difference. Thank you for your astute editing, along with the entertaining notes you made in the margins. Here's to a fourth book together!

And thank you, Beena Kamlani, for your insightful comments. Despite your demanding schedule, you made time to read, then reread, my manuscript, filling in all the holes with your discerning insight.

Big thanks to my indispensable support team, my wonderful friends who kept my life clicking while I was consumed with writing. Linda Lockwood, you're much more than an accountant, you're a lifesaver. Janey Anderson, Monica Mick Hager, and Ray Weber, thanks for keeping my home beautiful and in great shape, and Dacia Morrisonbuck, many thanks for your creative, mouth-watering treats every week. Eileen Michaels, I deeply appreciate your continuing guidance, not only with investments, but with everything else, especially our friendship.

Arlene Mikelson, great job typing the transcripts. Kristy Hood and Andrew Koijane, because of you I have the perfect Tahoe house where I wrote the last chapter. Dave Conklin, you performed miracles with your camera. Jane Champion, thank you so much for creating wonderful videos, and for the many more to come! And big thanks to the team at Electric Arrow for building a Web site that was just what I wanted.

How do I thank the three most important people in my life, my daughters, Anna, Julie, and Melissa? You are, each in your own way, my inspiration, my teachers, my closest friends, and without doubt, my biggest supporters!! I love you more than words can say.

I love you too, Mom. You've always been a proud mother, the self-appointed captain of my cheerleading squad. Now you've also become my role model. You faced a stunning loss with unbelievable grace, dignity, power, and strength. I always knew you had it in you.

Then there's my extended family: Gwen and Cliff Knoll, Beth Stanny, and Brenda and John Insull. I cherish your continued presence in my life. You're more important to me than you could possibly know and I truly love each of you.

If it wasn't for the hundreds of Overcoming Underearning™ workshop participants, who candidly shared their journey with me, and allowed me to share theirs in these pages, this book would not have seen the light of day. I know your stories will motivate many others. I genuinely appreciate your time, and am awed by your commitment.

And Daddy, a very special thank you . . . I *know* you're still with me.

A Parable

BY BARBARA STANNY

"We have enough people who tell it like it is. Now we could use a few who tell it like it could be."

—Robert Orben

Once upon a time there was a farmer who lived at the edge of a forest where a horrible monster dwelled. The monster was mean, ugly, and threatened to destroy everything. To protect himself, the farmer built walls around his property. But no matter how high the walls the farmer built, or how strong they were, the monster tore them down.

One day the farmer sat at his hearth, poking the embers, trying to spark a flame. He was cold and he was tired.

"My life has become unmanageable," he thought. "All I do is build and rebuild walls. My crops are dying. My wife and children have left. My friends rarely come around, and those who do only complain about the monster. I'm tired of living like this. I can't take it anymore . . ."

At that very moment, a Fairy Godmother appeared. She introduced herself to the farmer, and offered him a wish.

"I want the monster to go away," the farmer cried immediately.

"I can't make monsters disappear," she told him. "But I can show you how to do it."

"Anything, I'll do anything," the farmer exclaimed.

"You must go into the woods and find the monster," the Fairy Godmother said. "Then look it in the eye and embrace it."

The farmer was horrified. "I can't do that. It'll kill me."

"It's already killing you," the Fairy Godmother said gently.

The farmer was silent. She was right. He had little to lose. "All right," he said firmly. "I'll do it."

"Know this," the Fairy Godmother said. "You won't be alone." And in an instant, she was gone.

The farmer was frightened but determined. Off he went into the woods. Deeper and deeper he traveled.

"This is crazy," he thought, pushing back branches. "I've spent my whole life trying to keep the monster away, and now I'm going looking for it. How do I know this will work? Why am I taking this risk?"

He was just about to turn back when he heard a fierce growl, felt the earth tremble, and there, miles above him, loomed the most hideous creature he had ever seen. The farmer stood frozen. He wanted to run back to his walls, back to the safety of his cold, lonely cabin. But something kept him there, and he knew what it was. His pain had gotten worse than his fear.

So he looked up, right into the monster's eyes, and something amazing happened. The monster started shrinking. Smaller and smaller it grew until it was no bigger than he was. Then the farmer went over and touched it, cautiously.

"Embrace it," he heard the words echo from a distance.

The farmer took a deep breath and put his arms around the monster's neck, tentatively at first, then more willingly. And to his surprise, the monster became so tiny it could fit in the palm of his hand. He scooped it up and stared at it. It was no longer a threat. But the farmer had a sudden thought. What if it grows back?

Again, he heard the reassuring voice. "When you learn to face what makes you fearful, it need never control you again."

At last, the farmer was free, and all the energy he had put into building walls was his for building a new life. His shoulders grew straighter. A smile cracked his face. "I had this power all along," he realized in amazement. "Imagine what's possible now!"

And the voice whispered back, "Believe me, this is only the beginning . . ."

Finding Freedom

"And how do you keep your feet on the ground/
When you know that you were born . . . to fly?"

—Words from "Born to Fly," a country-western song

MY STORY

Money has always been my slippery slope. I didn't get a grip on managing it until my mid-forties, and only then after disaster struck. Making it took another decade.

Growing up, my father, Richard Bloch, the cofounder of H&R Block, had only one piece of financial advice for me: "Don't worry." The meaning was unmistakable: "You have a trust fund, and besides, a man will take care of you." By gender and generation, it was how he'd been brought up, and he honestly believed it. So did I . . . eagerly. The accepted wisdom for men of his age was that women didn't need to understand finances; in fact, the less they knew, the better. And that was fine with me. I wasn't interested in understanding money. I just wanted to spend it.

Now I know better. I'm convinced *if you don't deal with your money, your money will deal with you* . . . often in ways you'd never expect.

That's how it was for me. Neither my father nor I expected that my husband—a financial advisor by profession—would lose a substantial portion of my inheritance; that after our divorce, I'd get a million-dollar bill for taxes he hadn't paid, illegal deals he'd got us into. And I certainly never expected, when I asked my father to lend me money for those back tax bills, that he'd say no.

I realize now that his refusal was the best thing he could've done for me. But at the time I was furious. Even more, I was terrified. Suddenly, my secure little world was swirling out of control. I was alone in treacherous waters, wondering how in the hell I'd ever keep myself and my three daughters afloat. For months, I drifted in a daze, punctuated by waves of icy panic. It felt so unfair. Eventually, however, I got fed up with fear and self-pity. My children were my motivation. I knew that staying stupid was not an option. I had to get smart, and get smart fast!

Fortunately, I found a very astute financial counselor, Karen McCall. Unfortunately, I refused to listen to what she had to say.

"You're an underearner," she told me quite bluntly.

I wasn't quite sure what she meant. She explained that I've been earning way below what I should be making. If she said more, I didn't hear it. A white-hot bolt of shame ripped through me. I felt naked, as if my incompetence had been exposed for the world to see. My knee-jerk reaction was to go on the defensive.

"I am *not* an underearner," I insisted. "I'm a writer!" This made perfect sense to me. Everyone knows writers don't make any money.

Being labeled an underearner was so embarrassing that I ignored her advice, and instead dove headfirst into the bewildering world of finance, determined to get back on my feet with the money I had left. I took classes, read books, consulted professionals, watched money shows on TV, but to no avail. My brain fogged up, my eyes glazed over. I felt hopelessly stupid. Then destiny intervened (as it frequently does when you're *really* committed). I was hired for a project to research financially savvy women. Simply from interviewing those smart women, I not only figured out how to manage the money I had left, but I became an expert on empowering women around the subject of money. I wrote a book, *Prince Charming Isn't Coming: How Women Get Smart About Money*, and traveled the country teaching financial education to women.

But no matter how hard I worked—I worked long and hard, you can ask my three daughters—I could not seem to make much money. (Of course, I still clung to that starving-writers myth.)

Then one day my agent, Candice Fuhrman, called with a book idea: interview women who are making a lot of money. I immediately hated it. I pictured cold, aloof, designer-dressed snobs, leagues above me, totally intimidating if not downright boring. Then it hit me. If this is what I thought of successful women, how would I ever let myself become one? This was my first inkling that my own beliefs could be holding me back.

In March 2000 I began researching *Secrets of Six-Figure Women: Surprising Strategies to Up Your Earnings and Change Your Life*. I interviewed 154 high-earners, several of whom were writers. There went my pretext, along with my preconceptions. These women were wonderful, not at all what I had expected. They were indeed supremely confident, *but*—this was startling to me—every single one grappled with fear and self-doubt. Many felt like a fraud and were afraid others would find out. I could completely relate. The biggest difference between them and me, I realized, is that they didn't let self-doubt stop them. Instead, they employed a series of strategies I was hearing about for the very first time. That's when I began leading Overcoming Underearning™ workshops to field-test what I was learning from these high earners, to see if these strategies could empower others as well.

In the middle of this research, a miracle occurred. My accountant informed me I had earned six figures, and I hadn't even finished writing the book. Without even realizing it, I had seamlessly incorporated their strategies into my life, which I'll share with you throughout this book. And the workshops became a powerful and often life-altering experience for those who participated.

BRIDGING THE GENDER GAP

This book grew out of those workshops. *Overcoming Underearning: A Five-Step Plan to a Richer Life* began as a series of handouts, stapled together, distributed to small groups of women who gathered in my home. I gradually added more information, organized the pages into a spiral-bound workbook, rented space in restaurants or office buildings, and began drawing women from all over the country. The attendees bought workbooks for family and friends. Buoyed by the positive feedback I was getting, I expanded the workbook, filled it with new material and real-life examples, shaping it into the book you are now reading.

The workshops, like my books, were originally for women. I never expected to hear from so many men who read my books, used my workbook, and told me how much they had gained. Clearly, underearning crosses gender lines.

The wage gap may favor men, but dissatisfaction with earnings and worry about the future is a source of stress for both sexes. Underearning—or earning below one's potential—is a pervasive condition that affects millions of people, with symptoms ranging from a mild lack of fulfillment to a life of hardship and unhappiness.

★ Fifty percent of all Americans, men *and* women, feel underpaid (www.careerpath.com).
★ Fifty-nine percent of both men and women believe they are not paid as much as their peers in similar jobs (*New York Times*, October 2, 2002).
★ Forty-two percent of women and 32 percent of men worry about not having enough money (Prudential Financial Survey, 2004).
★ Only 35 percent of men and just 28 percent of women ever expect to get rich (Gallup, 2002).
★ "Men in jobs held mostly by women are also victims of pay bias" (Cornell Study, 2002).

My purpose in writing this book is to keep you from becoming (or staying) one of those statistics. With that in mind, I've written this book for men as well as women. Yet, for simplification (or perhaps out of habit), I tend to use the pronoun "she" more often. Also, since my interviews for this book were primarily with workshop alums, the examples given will be predominantly female. Still, I guarantee, readers of both sexes will benefit equally from the book, for the five steps to overcome underearning apply to everyone.

MOVE INTO THE DRIVER'S SEAT

My intent for this book, as it is for the workshops, is not just to help you put more cash in the bank. I know for a fact that when you start taking control of your money, you start taking control of your life.

I remember my interview with Jason Beckett, whose wife attended an early workshop and introduced him to the material. Jason was a manager of a big-box discount store. Like many others, he had never thought of himself as an underearner before. He just figured he didn't make enough money.

He also shared another trait common among underearners: the feeling of being trapped in an unsatisfying situation, convinced he had no choice.

"I knew that I had so much more potential, that I was never going to be happy doing what I was doing, and as a retail manager I was limited in what I could earn," he told me. But he didn't know how to change, or if it was even possible.

Did the strategies from the workshop make a difference? I asked. "Without doubt!" he replied enthusiastically. "It was liberating." In his spare time, Jason, an artist, designed innovative pieces of furniture. He was in the midst of negotiating a contract with a major furniture distributor to design a line of chairs, tables, and ottomans. The principles in the workbook freed him to follow his passion as an artist and make money doing it as a business.

"The fundamental difference, for me," he explained, "was to realize that *I actually have the power to affect who I am and how I live.*"

This book is designed to do the same for you—to show you that you have the power to control your life. The process is not complex. I've conceived it as a simple five-prong plan that we'll proceed through together, step-by-step, in Section 2.

YOU'RE HOLDING A HYBRID IN YOUR HANDS

Overcoming Undereaming™ is part book, part workbook, part journal— a combination self-study guide and bedside diary. It is meant to be an interactive experience, as if you were attending one of my workshops. I recommend reading it with a highlighter handy, along with a pen or pencil to respond to the self-evaluation tools included throughout.

As a Book. . . .

You'll learn about underearning: what it is, how it affects you, why you're susceptible, and most important, how to overcome it. You'll discover five simple, powerful steps that can move you from underearning to the next level in your life, wherever that may be for you.

As a Journal. . . .

If you jot down your thoughts as you go along, you'll create a personal record of your changing relationship to money. Each chapter is structured to track your progress as you read, respond to the exercises, and reflect on your reactions. There is limited space for journaling in this book. I encourage you to also have a separate journal, or notebook, for longer musings. I believe, based on my interviews, you'll find your personal ruminations the most profound and revealing feature in the book.

As a Workbook. . . .

You'll get the most value by doing the exercises, checklists, questionnaires, and visualizations. These tools allow you to zero in on your unique obstacles, adapt each step to your own situation, and create a personalized action plan for long-term change.

Every chapter ends with a recap or Highlights of the major points, and a space for reflection that I call "Conversation with Myself." In **Conversation,** you'll be asked specific questions related to the chapter's theme. You can respond to the questions offered, or write about whatever is in your heart. You'll learn a lot about yourself in this exercise, and you'll be able to observe your changes as you reread what you write.

It's easy to forget valuable insights, so as you go through this workbook, jot down your ideas as they occur.

Overcoming Underearning™ is divided into three sections:

★ Section 1, "Getting Started," explains how to use this book for the best results, and lays the groundwork for breaking through your earning barriers.

★ Section 2, "Taking the Steps," moves chapter by chapter through each of the five steps necessary to overcome underearning.

★ Section 3, "Ensuring Success," shows you how to create an ongoing plan to make sure you stay on track long after you've come to the last page.

THE PROMISE OF THIS BOOK

No matter what your gender, age, occupation, or economic bracket, the message I hope you take away is this: Underearning is not a life sentence. Overcoming it is more in your control than you realize. It's never too late to start. And the reward for your efforts will go far beyond money.

Conversation with Myself

To get you started: How do you feel about working with this book? What are your immediate reactions or concerns? What would it look like if you had control over your life? Why do you think the parable about the farmer and the monster was included in a book about overcoming underearning?

Getting Started

"Man's main task in life is
to give birth to himself,
to become what he
potentially is."

—Erich Fromm

"If we did all the
things we're capable of
doing, we would literally
astonish ourselves."

—Thomas Edison

ONE

Laying the Groundwork

"Life is not about finding yourself.
Life is about creating yourself."

—*George Bernard Shaw*

SOMEDAY IS NOW

How often have you found yourself thinking, "I wish I made more money?" Only to add with a sigh, "Someday . . . maybe someday . . ."

Guess what? *There is no someday.* This is it! This is the day to start turning your vague desire into a deep-seated commitment. This is the day to shift from building castles in the air to laying a solid foundation. This is the day you will start breaking through your barriers and bolster your earnings.

"Your aspirations are your possibilities."

—*Samuel Johnson*

THE SPILL-OVER EFFECT

It would be wonderful if, upon reading this book, you went straight into making six figures. And that may happen. Or not. Some of you may already be making six figures and still be underearning. I see it all the time—people who are professionally successful, yet financially strapped. Earning six figures is not a sure sign you've reached your earning potential. Nor is it the intent of this book. The real purpose is to help you achieve financial independence.

Financial Independence

You have the resources to live a satisfying, comfortable life, accomplish your dreams and goals, and have more fun doing what you do.

Life as an underearner is *not* a lot of fun. Being underpaid is frustrating, at best, and often debilitating. Underearning limits your choices, your freedom, your peace of mind, and your quality of life.

Maybe you can't make six figures, at least not right away. But you *can* make more than you're making now. And you can do it without selling your soul, no matter what circumstances you find yourself in. And it won't be just your bank account that benefits. In these pages you will meet people who ended up with far more than material wealth.

"My whole life has changed substantially," massage therapist Cheri Schell declared during our follow-up interview.

Within six months after taking the Overcoming Underearning™ workshop, she had increased her income by 20 percent, cut her hours "way back," lost twenty-three pounds, stopped using credit cards, started saving, moved to a nicer office, redecorated her home, saw her marriage improve, and had more time to herself.

"I'm making more, working less, feeling healthier, have more energy, and I'm so much happier."

"Desire is the starting point of all achievement . . ."

—Napoleon Hill

Cheri was not an exception. I was amazed how many reported significant changes in all areas of their lives. Aside from **increased income,** the most common "side effects" of the workshop were—in this order—**significant weight loss, better financial habits, more leisure time, improved health, increased optimism,** and **enhanced relationships.**

YOUR TURN

This whole process begins with one simple question: **What do you want?** At this point in my workshops, I always ask participants to think about why they came, what they wish to achieve. I'd like you to do the same. Take a moment to think about what you hope to accomplish from using this book. What drew you to it? Here are some examples of what other people have described as their goals:

- ★ Stop using credit cards.
- ★ Get out of debt.
- ★ Clarify my vision.
- ★ Make more money without losing myself.
- ★ Find out what's stopping me.
- ★ Get over feeling "I'm too old."

- ★ Take myself more seriously.
- ★ In my business, I want to see black instead of red.
- ★ Start saving for retirement.
- ★ Quit my job.
- ★ Overcome my fear.
- ★ Earn really big money.

BECOMING A GOAL GETTER

When you set goals, you are making things happen by focusing your attention, determining your choices, shaping outcomes, and attracting opportunities to fulfill those objectives. "Inherent in every desire is the mechanics for its fulfillment," author and physician Deepak Chopra tells us. The clearer you are about what you want, the greater your chances are to achieve it. If you write your goals down, they are more likely to happen than if they're just stored in your head.

For some, setting goals is a piece of cake. For others, it's a major source of indigestion. Few underearners, especially women, ever ask themselves: What do I want? And when they do, they often have a very tough time coming up with an answer.

That's usually because they're too busy worrying about what everyone else wants. And if they do acknowledge their own needs, they often dismiss them as selfish, silly, or even too grandiose.

Write Your Goals Here

Most of us fail to realize that self-denial, while seemingly virtuous, can lead to anger, resentment, pain, and sometimes illness. Not exactly conducive for monetary, or any other, success.

So, in the box above, write down everything you wish to occur from reading this book, no matter how ridiculous, outrageous, unreasonable, or even mundane it may seem. The following exercise may give you some additional insight.

Exercise: Six Months to Live

This can be a very eye-opening exercise. In fact, it was after doing this very exercise that I decided to become a writer. Before you answer the questions, get very quiet, close your eyes, and imagine this scene: the doctor has just told you that you only have six months to live. Take time to absorb the fact that your time on earth is limited, to visualize exactly how you'd want to spend those last few days.

If you knew you had six months to live,
What would you be doing?

Where would you be living?

Who would you be with?

What would you change? What would you add? What would you eliminate?

Why don't you start right now, living as if you only had six months left? The truth is, all of us have only a limited time on this planet. The purpose of this exercise is to encourage you to live that life to the fullest.

If you still can't think of anything, make something up. You can always go back and change it.

Share what you've written with at least one other person who will be supportive. Sure, telling people your goals takes guts, but it's worth it. A written goal that is also spoken has an even greater likelihood of being achieved. Besides, declaring what you want is mandatory for higher earnings, so consider this good practice.

> "Make your plans as fantastic as you like, because twenty-five years from now they will seem mediocre. You will wonder why you didn't make them 50 times as great."
>
> —*Henry Curtis*

My Goals for You

I had five particular goals in mind when I wrote this book, five outcomes I hope to help you achieve. I want to:

1. CHANGE YOUR RELATIONSHIP WITH MONEY.
   It can be life altering when you start viewing your financial issues not as a source of shame, but as a tool for personal growth, a doorway to new possibilities.
2. EXPLORE YOUR BLOCKS AND BARRIERS TO SUCCESS. This can only happen if you do the exercises thoughtfully and reflectively.
3. INSPIRE YOU TO THINK BIGGER. It's time to replace a bake-sale mentality with a grander vision about how much you can make and how much more you can be. As writer Marianne Williamson says, "Your playing small doesn't serve the world."
4. KEEP YOU ON THE PATH. Goals are not attainable all at once. There will be barriers, dead ends, and frustrating

continued

periods when it seems as if nothing is happening. My goal is to make sure you stay on course.

5. ENCOURAGE YOU TO SHARE WHAT YOU LEARN. Not only can you help other people with everything you've discovered, but you strengthen what you share. Believe me, no one learns more than the teacher.

A FEW WORDS ABOUT DOING THE EXERCISES IN THE WORKBOOK

★ Don't try to find "the perfect answer." There's no such thing.

★ Don't think too much. It's best to write the first thought that comes to mind.

★ More important than your initial response is what the questions trigger later. Your most valuable insights may come when you're falling asleep or taking a shower.

★ After doing each exercise, write what you discover in this book or in a separate journal. Then call a friend to discuss your findings and feelings. Discussion almost always leads to further insight.

NOT A ONE PERSON SHOW

"Tell me, I forget.
Show me, I remember.
Involve me, I understand."

—*Chinese proverb*

I highly recommend doing the exercises with other people—your spouse or partner, friends, colleagues, or family members. If you can't meet in person, discuss your findings over the phone or online. When I asked women what they valued most about the workshop, practically everyone responded that they loved the support, the insights—those they themselves had as well as contributions from others—and the sense of relief they felt listening to others describe what they themselves had felt but never talked about. "I never knew anyone else felt this way. I'm not alone!" they'd say, as if that awareness itself was worth the price of admission.

These Are People I'd Like to Work With

Jot down a few names you'd like to share this work with, and then contact them. Ask if they'd be willing to travel on this journey with you.

DON'T LISTEN TO BLANCHE

I'll never forget one workshop, when we went around the room and shared our goals for the day. One woman, Leanne Kramer, declared hers was "to make Blanche shut up." **Blanche?** "That's the voice in my head," she explained, "that tells me I'm not smart enough." With that, another woman blurted out, "Mine is Sister Mary Margaret, the nun who told me I'd never amount to anything."

We all have our Blanches or Mary Margarets. "They were the messages I gave myself and had accepted up to that point," Sally Beckett said. " 'It's okay to work so hard and not get paid; everybody else comes first, the left-overs are for you.' It's very hard to get rid of those messages. I deal with them over and over in different disguises."

> "You'll never amount to anything."
>
> —Einstein's Greek teacher

Those voices may never shut up. Mine haven't. In fact, I found a passage in the journal that I kept while writing *Secrets of Six-Figure Women*: "There's this nagging little voice, way back in my head—more a feeling than a voice: 'you shouldn't want money. You shouldn't be telling others to want it either. It's bad, It's wrong.' It's like a finger wagging at me, 'Bad girl. You shouldn't be after money.' "

Those voices still sneer at me from time to time. I've learned to ignore them. So should you. *Just because you hear voices in your head doesn't mean you have to listen to them.*

Don't argue with the voice, or attempt to silence it. You probably can't if you try. What you resist persists, and only gets louder. Let it rant. Observe what it says. Keep reminding yourself: that's not *my* voice. It's the voice of a parent, the culture, teachers, friends, something "out there." But it isn't yours. My advice? Simply say "Thank you for sharing," and do what you need to do.

> "If you hear a voice within you say 'you cannot paint,' by all means paint, and that voice will be silenced."
>
> —Vincent van Gogh

Start replacing the voices with different, more positive statements, a personal mantra or affirmation. My mantra became: "Money is wonderful. I am helping people have better lives." I'd say it over and over, until the internal barrage of criticism faded away, at least for the moment.

Jody Stevenson realized her inner voices kept insisting "Money destroys families," a belief that sprang from past experience. She wrote out two affirmations: Money enhances families. Money brings joy to families.

"I'd say them all the time, while driving or shopping. They became my mantras. It worked. I absolutely know now that money supports families." I don't believe it's an accident that her income quickly went up $2,500 a month.

THE OTHER VOICE . . .

You also have another voice, a much more authentic one. Call it your soul, your higher self, your inner wisdom—or even your fairy godmother. Sometimes it's hard to hear. Other times, you may not want to listen. But I truly believe it's the part of you that has put this book in your hands, that wants to become more of who you are, live the life you were meant to live, and make a difference in the world. Much of the work we'll be doing in the following pages will be finding that authentic inner voice, turning up the volume, and beginning to trust what it tells us.

> "Freedom, by definition, is people realizing that they are their own leaders."
>
> —*Diane Nash,*
> *civil rights activist*

CHAPTER ONE HIGHLIGHTS

* ★ The purpose of *Overcoming Underearning*™ is to achieve **Financial Independence**—to live a comfortable satisfying life, accomplish your dreams and goals, and have more fun.
* ★ The results you can expect go way beyond money, from losing weight to gaining more leisure time to improved relationships.
* ★ The process begins by asking yourself this question: What do I want?
* ★ Ignore Blanche, the critical voice in your head.
* ★ Instead, start tuning into your **Authentic Voice,** the one who genuinely knows what you're capable of becoming.

Conversation with Myself

Practice listening to the "Blanches" in your head. How have they affected your life and others so far? Can you distinguish between Blanche and your Authentic Voice? What are each saying about the goals you wrote down? What else do you suspect your Authentic Voice may be telling you?

Now, turn the page and take the quiz.

Underearning Quiz

Are you an underearner? Let's find out. Circle the numbers of the statements that apply to you. Do this quickly, without thinking too much about your response. Circle the ones that might apply even if you're not quite sure.

1. I often give away my services (volunteering, or working more hours than I'm actually paid).
2. It's so hard to ask for a raise (or to raise fees) that I just don't do it.
3. I actually dislike money and/or the people who have it.
4. I am proud of my ability to make do with little. There's nobility in being poor.
5. I blame someone or something else for my financial situation (IRS, ex-husband).
6. I find ways to avoid dealing with money (bartering, credit cards).
7. I tend to sabotage myself at work (apply for jobs not qualified for or low-paying, stop short of reaching goals, change jobs a lot.)
8. I work very, very hard (long hours, several jobs). Or I go into excess and then collapse.
9. I fill my free time with endless chores and tasks.
10. I am in debt, with little savings, and no idea where my money is going.
11. I have a family history of debt and/or underearning.
12. I am vague about my earnings (overestimate or underestimate income; see gross, not net).
13. I continually put others' needs before my own.
14. I am frequently in pain or stress around money.
15. Recognition and praise are more important to me than money.
16. I am confident in my ability to make money.
17. I always live below my means.
18. I love money and appreciate what it does for me.
19. I am very optimistic about my financial future.
20. I experience very little fear or insecurity around money.
21. I am determined to get paid what I am worth.
22. I am passionate about my work.
23. I have very supportive, nurturing relationships (including spouse).
24. I like wealthy people.
25. I have little or no credit card debt.

continued

26. I intentionally get myself in situations beyond my ability and then rise to them.
27. I am resilient and able to bounce back when I fail.
28. I am filled with gratitude for the success I've achieved.
29. I work very hard, but I know I don't have to do everything myself. I know how to delegate and set limits.
30. I am tenacious in achieving my goals.

If you circled two or more of statements 1 through 15, you're probably earning less than your potential, despite your efforts and/or desire to make more.

If you circled two or more of statements 16 through 30, you're likely in the upper-income brackets of your profession or industry. Or you should be. Are you ready to go even higher?

Even if you qualify as a hard-core underearner, you probably have at least a few high-earning traits (statements 16 through 30). The point of this work is to strengthen and expand those, while eliminating the others.

What I discovered:

Creating Affirmations

Use the last fifteen statements on the quiz as affirmations.
Affirmations are positive statements used to program your
subconscious. Write them down. Say them out loud. Repeat
them over and over again, every day, until you begin to
believe it. (See appendix for more affirmations.)

TWO

Are You an Underearner?

*"Work your fingers to the bone, what do you get?
Boney fingers. Boney fingers."*

—Hoyt Axton, country singer

ARE YOU OR AREN'T YOU?

Once, during a workshop break, an adorable thirty-five-year-old pony-tailed Filipino woman came up and tapped me on the shoulder. Her name was Odette D'Aniello. She looked genuinely confused.

"I'm not sure I'm an underearner," she said. "I own a bakery that's very profitable."

"Then what's the problem?" I replied.

"I hardly pay myself anything," she said. "It's how I was taught. You have to put everything back into the business so you can weather any storms."

"You're definitely an underearner," I assured her.

It's common for people to doubt, even debate, whether they actually belong in this category. "I'm not an underearner," they'll contend. "I just don't make enough money." For some, it's denial. The term isn't exactly flattering. For others, it's fear of change.

"If I admitted that I was an underearner," a friend once divulged, "then I would need to do something about it."

But mostly they're uninformed. The traits are not widely known. The term isn't even in the dictionary. Figuring out if the label fits can be a little tricky.

YOUR FIRST CLUE

All underearners, without question, share one common trait: *a high tolerance for low pay.* This is a sure sign of underearning. Yet even that description doesn't tell the whole story. "Low pay" is a relative term. You can make six figures and still be an underearner. Conversely, you can earn far less and not fit that category.

Don't let the term fool you. Underearners can be hard to spot.

"I was amazed to be in a room with such poised, professional women who looked successful, who made so much more money than I did, yet still considered themselves underearners," observed Teresa Fanucchi, age thirty-six. "That really played with my perception of what it meant to be an underearner."

What does it mean to be an underearner? To start with, it has little to do with the amount of money you make. It has everything to do with your attitude.

What Underearning Is . . . and Isn't

DEFINITION OF UNDEREARNER: One who earns less than her potential despite her need or desire to do otherwise.

UNDEREARNING is not the same as VOLUNTARY SIM-PLICITY, which is a conscious choice to live on less in order to create a simpler, saner life.

continued

> An UNDEREARNER is not the same as A MINDFUL LOW
> EARNER, someone who enjoys her work because it feeds her
> soul and also provides adequate income.
>
> Underearning is a condition of DEPRIVATION in which your
> emotional and/or physical needs are not being met.

Underearning is rarely a conscious choice. It never leads to a saner or more satisfying life. It always involves self-denial—not only of money, but time, freedom, impact, and joy; denial of your value, your power, your needs, and your options.

TALE OF TWO WOMEN

Here are two examples of women making less than their potential. Both could be considered underearners. Can you see why they're not?

> "... a condition of ulti-
> mate deprivation, that is,
> poverty."
>
> —*Dante's definition of Hell*

Katherine Brennan Murphy left a corporate job in a high-tech company making $80,000 to start a consulting business. It was well on its way to becoming very successful when she took a sabbatical to care for her mother, who had suddenly become ill. Now she's ready to get into consulting again.

Katherine is convinced, based on the going rates for her level of expertise, that she can make good money as an entrepreneur. If not, she'll seek out corporate work.

"I'm not earning anything yet, but it's out of choice," she explained. "I'm giving myself eighteen months. I know I'm worth $120,000. But I may choose to earn less if I find work that's fulfilling, of service to others, and would give me economic security."

Jean Hamilton is the owner of Speaking Results, a thriving business that offers speaking and presentation training to individuals and executives. She's also the mother of two young children. She makes a very good living, contributes significantly to the family's income, and has great confidence in her earning potential. But she consciously opted, in the beginning, to grow her business and her income slowly. Now that her youngest is in school, she's picking up the pace.

"One thing I feel very proud of," she said, "is that I've been able to balance motherhood and career very well." She's with the kids after school every day and puts them to bed every night.

"I used to be a performing artist," she recalled. "And for years I lived with the feeling that I could never earn a lot of money. I just thought earning a lot of money was for other people, not me. Then something shifted when I started this company. I knew that if I set out to earn a good income, I could do it."

What shifted was her attitude. Hers, like Katherine's, is very different from your typical underearner's. Both these women made a conscious choice to live on less without depriving or devaluing themselves. They still benefited from the Overcoming Underearning™ workshop, because it helped them clarify their focus, strengthen their intentions, learn additional tools, and increase their sense of value. It will do the same for you, too. Even if you're not a bona fide underearner, the principles in this book will definitely help you get ahead. The bonus for you is that it'll probably be a lot easier to apply them.

> "Money frees you from doing things you dislike. Since I dislike doing nearly everything, money is handy."
>
> —*Groucho Marx*

Let's look at the major characteristics of an underearner (somewhat revised since first published in *Secrets of Six-Figure Women*). Can you relate to any of them?

TEN TRAITS OF UNDEREARNERS

1. Underearners talk as if they're trapped.

Underearners feel stuck, as if they have no control over their lives or their time. And they truly believe it. They justify, defend, or rationalize their situations with an array of excuses that block out their options with emotional blinders. They can't see past where they stand. And when they do, they don't like what they see.

I vividly remember a teacher in one workshop becoming almost combative. "I can't leave what I do. I'm raising a daughter. I'm not trained for anything else. I'm not going back to college or type someone's memos. I don't want to have to struggle, start at square one, and work all the time."

"You're painting an awfully dismal picture," I told her. But what got her attention were the two former teachers who had transferred their skills into fulfilling careers. One works for an educational consulting firm; the other is a technical writer.

2. Underearners give their power away.

No wonder underearners feel trapped. They're constantly projecting their power "out there." They blame other people or outside conditions for causing their problems. Or they wait, hoping someone or something will come in and save them. Prince Charming is a favorite for women; the lottery ranks high for both genders.

"I spent my whole life waiting for my shining knight," chuckled a middle-aged woman, who was getting married for the first time. Then with a sigh, she added, "He came without a bankroll." So she came to the workshop.

As long as you believe the locus of control lies outside of yourself, all attempts to overcome underearning will be halfhearted or misdirected.

3. Underearners underestimate their worth.

Underearners give away their time, knowledge, skills, experience for free or bargain prices because they don't believe they're worth more.

"It never occurred to me I could make six figures," a graphic artist admitted. "I don't feel like what I do is good enough to make all that money. It's that old 'I'm not worthy' thing."

She described a recent negotiation with a client. You could see others, nodding their heads, had done the same. "I told him my rates were $35, but in the next breath, I said, 'For you I'll do it for $25 an hour.' I didn't even give him a chance to react."

Because they devalue themselves, underearners instinctively settle for less or seek their value by volunteering, in the job or outside of it. There's nothing wrong with pro bono work—in fact, it's a wonderful gift to those in need—as long as it's on top of an already satisfying, well-paying job.

Mikelann Valterra, author of *Why Women Earn Less*, puts it like this: "If someone is saying I wish I made more money and giving their time away for free, there's a disconnect there."

Volunteering feels good, but it's a poor substitute for financial well-being, and it can become a form of self-sabotage, drawing you away from income-producing work. As a database administrator told me, "Most of my recognition comes from taking on different projects here at work, stuff that doesn't pay, but gives me lots of pats on the back." She didn't realize she could have pats on the back *and* the big bucks by doing jobs that were personally rewarding but also adequately compensated.

4. Underearners crave comfort.

I'll never forget my conversation with a man about his newfound success. "I feel like I'm walking around in someone else's body," he said. "I almost want to go back to my old me. This new one is so unfamiliar."

Change, even a dream come true, is rarely comfortable. Underearners will often unwittingly sabotage their success rather than endure the discomfort.

It's astonishing how fiercely we cling to our so-called comfort zones. What a misnomer. These places are anything but comfortable. They're just familiar and predictable.

I was particularly struck by Stephen's perceptive description of his lifelong pattern. "If I get too far below my comfort level, I make a big push to get more money. I'll go out and drum up business, call a friend who owes me money, whatever it takes. The reverse also happens. If I make a lot of money, I will spend my way back to my comfort level. Which is where I am now. I hate this comfort level, but it's almost as if the motivation isn't there to take me higher."

Stephen didn't realize he got something in exchange for his low pay, though at one point he practically admitted as much. "Living close to the edge gives me a sort of adrenaline rush. It goads me into action. But I don't like what it does to my life."

So why doesn't he just stop doing it? Most likely, he can't. Financial turmoil has become his drug of choice. Some people actually get hooked on the havoc wrought by underearning.

Often, beneath the underearner's inability to get ahead is a gaping emotional wound stemming from childhood trauma or more recent abuse. Underearning, like overspending, can be an unconscious attempt to numb the hurt. Financial tension becomes a perfect diversion from personal pain. But of course, as with all distractions, underearning never heals the ache. It only escalates it. Still, quitting an addiction requires massive discomfort.

5. Underearners are self-saboteurs.

People who underestimate their worth tend to undermine their success. That's why so many bright, talented people can't seem to get ahead. They unconsciously do things that make achievement impossible. They procrastinate, job hop, take on too much, become scattered and distracted. The list is endless.

"I am always giving away money," one woman told me. "I thought it was bad to be selfish." "I have so many interests," another said, "I can't just focus on one thing." And still another declared: "A client owes me a lot of money, but I'm just going to write it off." These are all people getting caught in their own subtle traps.

"My favorite self-sabotage is telling myself 'I can afford that,' " a woman told me. "I rationalize the hell out of why I need a $200 pair of shoes." She spoke for countless others. Frivolous or compulsive spending and debting are like quicksand. Once you get sucked in, you'll never make it to higher earnings until you start digging your way out.

6. Underearners are codependent.

People who don't value themselves easily slip into codependence, putting everyone else's needs before their own. While it may sound noble, taking care of others at your own expense is anything but admirable. Codependence creates victims.

"It's like I had this 'Use Me' sign on my forehead," said Elaine Hayes, describing her former job in a faith-based organization. "I'd drop everything for someone else, but I had no energy for myself. This is what happens in nonprofits. People give selflessly because they're passionate about the organization's mission. It's the norm. We believe to think otherwise is selfish."

This kind of thinking isn't limited to nonprofits. It's the typical mind-set of most underearners. Attending to everyone else before taking care of yourself is a form of self-sabotage and has been known to destroy careers, if not lives.

7. Underearners live in financial chaos.

When I ask people why they have come to the seminar, the typical reply is "I'm tired of working so hard and having nothing to show for it."

Underearners tend to live paycheck to paycheck, struggling to make ends meet, going from one financial crisis to another, racking up debt, working incessantly with no end in sight. This even applies to those who are making what sounds like good money.

Perhaps the biggest fear underearners have about earning more is that they'll have no life, that they'll be working all the time. What an irony! No one works harder or longer hours than an underearner.

Carney is a perfect example. She's a single mom, works two jobs putting in minimum twelve-hour days. "My life is ridiculously complicated. I'm working nonstop. I can't afford to hire someone to fix my dishwasher or clean my house. I have to do it. I spend all my 'free' time driving around looking for things on sale."

At some point the truth dawned on her: "You know, it's a lot harder work being an underearner than a high earner."

8. Underearners are vague about money and success.

Underearners use the same methods to manage their money as they do to make most decisions: avoidance and delusion. They often have no idea how much money they have, how much they earn, how much they owe, or even how much they need. They operate by wishful thinking instead of strategizing and negotiating, as high earners do.

And they are just as vague about why success eludes them. I often hear underearners say, as this woman did: "I'm smart. I'm good at what I do. Yet I'm always trying to get somewhere that I can't seem to get to. I really don't know why!"

9. Underearners are antiwealth.

During an interview with a woman who had made little progress, I asked her how much she'd like to be earning.

"I just don't want an obscene amount of money," she said.

"Why's that?" I inquired, not bothering to ask what she considered obscene.

"I never met a person with an obscene amount of money doing anything but obscene things."

Underearners can be terrible snobs. They're ambivalent or downright negative about money and/or people who have it. They dislike the wealthy, take great pride in living on a shoestring, believe there is virtue in being poor, and criticize those too focused on their finances.

As Carney said, "I was always so proud of my ability to make do with so little. But the workshop made me realize that the nobility of being poor was making my life a disaster."

Others are actually ashamed to admit money even matters. One person put it like this: "It's embarrassing to say you want to make money. A part of me thinks that if you want to help other people, it is selfish to want to make a lot of money doing it. Money is certainly not something I want to devote my life to."

And yet no one thinks more about money than an underearner. As one admitted during an interview, "If I earned more money, I wouldn't have to always think about it. I spend way too much time obsessing about where the money is going to come from."

10. Underearners are controlled by fear.

They're afraid of success. They're afraid of failing. They're afraid of rejection, of being judged, of people liking them (or not) because of their money. They're afraid of the responsibility of having more, and the possibility of losing it all. Some are afraid to even address their finances because "it's so grim and pointless it'll throw me into a tailspin," according to one. And another said: "I'm afraid of what I'll see in my future if I don't change my patterns." Yet she was having trouble changing for fear of the unknown. "And I know," she confessed, "I won't make any progress until I confront my fears." It is the catch-22 for all underearners. I have to change. I'm afraid to change. But confronting my fear is my only way out.

THE GOOD NEWS

Did you happen to notice what these ten traits all have in common? Every one of them is self-imposed. Every one is something we do to ourselves. Go back and reread each trait. Can you see how every one is the result of a choice we made? That's wonderful news. If we create the conditions for underearning to occur, we have the power to change them. Or as Barbara Christenson put it, "I saw underearning wasn't an out-of-control thing. Underearning was my responsibility."

> **"Don't blame the floor if you can't dance."**
> —*Source unknown*

BUT WAIT! IT'S NOT MY FAULT . . . .

Granted, stuff happens. There are indeed forces beyond our control that seem to dictate our life, determine our success: an unpredictable economy, a crowded job market, unforeseen emergencies, "bad luck," personal demands that usurp all our time. You're right. The unexpected is inevitable. Difficulties arise. Life gets in the way. We get sidetracked. Yet every high earner I've interviewed has faced these same forces and still came out ahead.

IF IT IS TO BE, IT'S UP TO ME . . .

This phrase could well be the high earner's motto. The simple decision to take responsibility for the state of your affairs can make all the difference, as bakery owner Odette will tell you.

"When I read the characteristics [of underearners], I thought 'Oh my God, that's me.' And I realized I created this for myself," Odette said. "I also realized I don't have to do this anymore. It's time to move on. I quit making the excuses I've made all these years. I decided I am worthy of earning more. My time is valuable. My talent is rare. I am going to earn much more than I've allowed myself."

She left the workshop and gave herself a $1,200 per month raise, began getting her baked goods into high-end groceries, studied profit margins for ways to cut costs, and over the next months met with investors to explore a major business expansion, and "continues to have flexibility to care for my two young children and nurture my loving marriage."

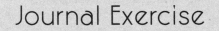

Journal Exercise

WHAT'S YOUR PAYOFF FOR UNDEREARNING?

Talk to the Underearner in you. Write about this in your own journal. Ask that part of yourself questions. See what it has to tell you. Why is it there? What's its purpose? Do you see that it has a gift for you? What have you gotten out of it?

She not only upped her income significantly, but she said the words I hear most often: "I feel so empowered." Empowering as it may be, however, taking responsibility can be as debilitating as it is liberating.

Eight months later, I got this e-mail from Odette: "We've doubled our sales and our accounts are growing. Our retail customer base is expanding so much that I've had to raise prices to control demand. And the demand keeps growing! My financial life is in tip-top shape. I get paid a lot more now both in time and money. We have no debt, and we have an extravagant Christmas trip to Maui planned and paid for."

THE DARK SIDE OF SELF-DETERMINATION

Long before all the glowing reports, however, I received an e-mail from Odette shortly after the workshop: "I wrote 8 pages in my giant journal cussing away at my choice of paying myself so little and continuing to underpay myself when I could have changed it. I am so angry."

I heard countless variations of this same response from so many others.

> "Disillusionment with yourself must precede Enlightenment."
>
> —*Vernon Howard*

"I did *not* like finding out I was responsible for underearning," exclaimed writer Sally Beckett. "It made me face that I was where I was because of my own actions, my own self-talk. It wasn't a capricious world smacking me on the side of the head."

She had two reactions. On one hand, she said: "I felt lost, like 'So what do I do now?' You feel like you're supposed to have the whole map of where you're supposed to go next, and you don't."

But on the other hand, she too felt empowered. "I sort of knew, in a vague way, what I'd been doing. Once I identified it, I knew I could do something about it. I just didn't know what."

You, too, can do something about it. We'll start by finding your internal barriers. Most of us have an earning ceiling. Let's see what the height of yours is, and more important, learn how to break through it.

CHAPTER TWO HIGHLIGHTS

★ An underearner is anyone who earns less than her potential, despite her need or desire to do otherwise.

★ Underearning is neither a conscious or satisfying choice, but a condition of deprivation (money, time, joy, freedom, choices).

★ Underearners
   1. talk as if they're trapped.
   2. give their power away.
   3. underestimate their worth.
   4. crave comfort.
   5. are self-saboteurs.
   6. are codependent.
   7. live in financial chaos.
   8. are vague about money and success.
   9. are antiwealth.
   10. are controlled by fear.

★ The good news: We have the power to change any of these traits.

Conversation with Myself

Would you call yourself an underearner? Why? What characteristics did you especially identify with? How do you feel knowing that you're responsible?

Discover Your Earnings Ceiling

CREATED BY KAREN MCCALL, FOUNDER OF THE FINANCIAL RECOVERY INSTITUTE
(WWW.FINANCIALRECOVERY.COM)

First, answer the following question. Write down the first number that pops into mind. Think in terms of what your services are worth, *not* what the market would pay.

How much do you want to make in a year? $ _____

Now get comfortable, relax your whole body, and picture yourself in a lovely, calm, serene setting. When you're ready, read the first line, then close your eyes and consider your answer. After a few seconds in meditation, open your eyes and write your response. Then read the next line and repeat.

Imagine you are earning $5,000 a year. How do you feel? What are your thoughts?

Imagine you are earning $10,000 a year. How do you feel? What are your thoughts?

Imagine you are earning $25,000 a year. How do you feel? What are your thoughts?

Imagine you are earning $50,000 a year. How do you feel? What are your thoughts?

Imagine you are earning $75,000 a year. How do you feel? What are your thoughts?

Imagine you are earning $100,000 a year. How do you feel? What are your thoughts?

Imagine you are earning $250,000 a year. How do you feel? What are your thoughts?

Imagine you are earning $500,000 a year. How do you feel? What are your thoughts?

Imagine you are earning $1,000,000 a year. How do you feel? What are your thoughts?

What did you discover? Were there any surprises? How high was your ceiling? What does this tell you?

Remember, there are no right or wrong answers to these exercises. The whole idea is to give you information about yourself. Did you have limitations? How did you feel when you saw them? Some people in my classes were thrilled to see they had no ceilings. Quite a few had no idea theirs were so low, while others were shocked theirs were so high. Here are some examples.

- ★ Ginger Moshofsky: "I realized that when I started getting too high, I started feeling 'Oooh, I'm not worth that.' When I got to $250,000, I thought, 'If I did, it would make me so uncomfortable.' Before this I would've sworn that I'd feel great. I never realized I had any discomfort around money."
- ★ Marilyn McCabe Love: "I was scared at the lower numbers. At $75,000, I started getting excited. $250,000 was fabulous. When I got to $500,000, I said, 'I'm worthy of this.' At that moment, I knew something had changed inside me. In the question, what did you discover, I wrote 'I deserve to be paid. I'm going to stop giving my skills away.' "
- ★ Janie Thomas: "I can say I want to make millions, but when I did this exercise, I felt the thud when I hit $75,000. It was a physical sensation. I could not imagine making that much."
- ★ Jolee Gestner: "Somewhere between $100,000 and $250,000 I lost my nerve. No way. I couldn't fathom it. My quality of life would be gone. I'd have to work all the time."

THREE

Breaking Through Your Earnings Barrier

"When a person acts without knowledge of what he thinks, feels, needs or wants, he does not yet have the option of choosing to act differently."

—*Clark Moustakas*

THE DAY IT DAWNED ON ME . . .

As some of you have no doubt discovered, the key to upping your earnings is rarely working longer hours or finding a scheme to get rich quick. And as my interviews have shown me, whatever direction the economy's going, there will always be people who are prospering. The fact is, the greatest hurdle to higher earnings, the *real* barrier, is rarely "out there."

I remember the moment I made that connection. The date was April 16, 2000. My research for *Secrets of Six-Figure Women* was well under way. I had just finished interviewing an executive whose annual income was over $1 million. While pondering her words, I had an epiphany! I grabbed my journal and began writing excitedly.

"No wonder I've never made much money. I've been tackling the problem from the wrong angle. I've been looking at what I need to *do*. No! I need to adjust my *thinking*."

I saw it so clearly. High earners thought differently from me. They weren't necessarily born that way. But somewhere along the line, they developed a certain mind-set, a totally different attitude that consistently showed up in every conversation. (Once, much later, I invited one of these successful women to an Overcoming Undearning™ workshop I was giving in Portland, Oregon, her hometown. Midway through the day, she leaned over and whispered, "I can't relate to anything these women are saying. I just don't think like that.")

> "What you do comes from what you think."
>
> —A Course in Miracles

Because high earners think differently, they make different choices and as a result produce very different outcomes. It wasn't my profession, I realized, or the business cycle, or whatever other excuses I had been conjuring up, that stood in my way. It was how I thought, pure and simple. If I had any hope of earning more, I knew I needed to fundamentally shift my thinking, to somehow reprogram my brain.

Up until then, I had been concentrating on what I should be doing (but wasn't), like ratcheting up my marketing, raising my fees, redoing my Web site. But I just couldn't seem to get myself going on any of these projects. Now I took a different tack. I made an appointment with a counselor and did many of the exercises you'll find in this book. Like oil separating from water, I began to distinguish the self-defeating thoughts I had been carrying since childhood, voices from my past I had adopted as my own. I heard my father say, "Making money is a man's job"; my mother declare, "Behind every successful man is a woman"; society whisper, "A man won't love you if you're too successful"; some faceless authority scold me, "It's bad to focus on money"; and my negative ego insist, "You do *not* have what it takes."

> "Traditionally, when a seeker goes to a master, one of the first things a master must do is break down the way the seeker sees the world."
>
> —Siddha Yoga

I had swallowed these toxic messages without thinking, coating my brain with limiting beliefs that kept tripping me up every step of the way.

As I became free of my past programming, my resistance to doing the "Outer Work" seemed to melt away. I found myself, almost effortlessly, creating a marketing plan, negotiating higher fees, hiring support staff, and finding a Web designer (actually he found me, sending me an e-mail out of the blue). Everything fell into place. From that point on, my income began its slow but steady rise.

THE SHIFT

Einstein explained it this way: "Our problems can't be solved at the same level of thinking we were at when we created them." It takes another level of thinking to break through our earning barriers, to solve our financial problems, too. Or as one woman in my seminar put it, "It's not just going through the steps. It's having a paradigm shift in your head."

Shifting a paradigm requires a two-pronged approach, a combination of the **Inner Work** and the **Outer Work.**

The Outer Work

The mechanics of marketing yourself, negotiating higher pay, and managing your money.

The Inner Work

Transforming your thoughts, feelings, beliefs, attitudes, and decisions about yourself and money.

There's no bypassing the latter. Regardless of how sophisticated or savvy you are, unless you address your internal blocks, you'll inadvertently sabotage your success.

CASE IN POINT: CONVERSATION WITH DONNA WEAVER, REAL ESTATE AGENT AND UNDEREARNER

Donna: I freeze and fog up around money. I just can't think about it. I hate dealing with it.

Me: But isn't real estate all about money?

Donna: Yeah, but the difference is, it's not about my money.

Me: So you're bewildered by your own finances and are crystal clear when dealing with other people's money?

Donna: And you know something? I'm positively brilliant with really complicated deals.

"Attitudes are more important than facts," famed psychiatrist Karl Menninger wisely noted. My six-figure women wholeheartedly agreed. "Attitude is everything," they always told me. It works like this: when you change your thoughts, your behavior follows. Irrational thinking will always undermine any attempts at rational behavior.

MIND OVER MONEY

I believe, as a culture, we have greatly underestimated the power of the mind when it comes to money. Years ago, one of the largest women's Web sites asked me to write a financial column, with one caveat. "Don't put in any of that touchy-feely stuff," they insisted.

Thankfully, that viewpoint is vanishing, albeit slowly. The *Wall Street Journal* recently pointed out, "The reason people get stuck is almost always an emotional reason . . . and they can get stuck for years . . . but the consequences are financial." And similarly, *Kiplinger's* reported, "Financial planners are increasingly finding themselves playing the role of psychologist as well as financial counselor."

> "The earning law stated is that: All wealth is created by the human mind. . . . Increasing your wealth is a matter of increasing the quality of your thoughts . . ."
>
> —*Phil Laut, author of* **Money Is My Friend**

Psychology is to money what an engine is to a car. Whenever you're stalled, that's the first place to look. But for some, the psyche is the last thing they want to deal with. It's just too complicated, too foreboding, too foreign. Yet looking "under the hood" is absolutely essential for attaining higher earnings.

If this isn't what you expected when you picked up this book, you're not alone. Quite a few people came to my workshops initially surprised that so much attention was paid to their emotions.

"I thought I signed up for a financial class and I ended up examining my own motives," one woman said. "It made me think a lot deeper than I expected."

Others were actually offended by this approach. "I was ticked off," Celt Schira, a registered professional electrical engineer, told me point-blank. "This stuff was pretty Zen. I wanted good hard skills on negotiating and selling myself."

Journal Exercise

How do you suppose the "quality of your thoughts" has affected your relationship with money?

But after the workshop, she acknowledged the value. "I've been better able to apply what I learned in the skill building classes. My business has increased. I'm a better negotiator. My income's gone up. *I think you have to get the insides straight before you can really consolidate the outer skills.*"

"Who looks outside, dreams. Who looks inside, awakens."

—*Carl Jung*

That's the whole point of doing the Inner Work—getting in shape to handle the heavy lifting of the Outer Work. Self-awareness is the missing link for anyone who's ever had trouble applying skills they've tried to learn, or doing the things they know they should to get ahead.

"The seminar wasn't what I expected at all," echoed Tami Mathisen. "I thought it was going to be about climbing the corporate ladder, not an emotional conversation. I walked away with a profound understanding that my relationship with money was all wrong. I walked away a different person."

Indeed, within a few months Tami had increased her income by $22,000, began building a home so her family could move out of a trailer, bought a new car, went back to school, tossed out forty bags of accumulated junk, and lost almost thirty pounds. (You'll read Tami's whole story in chapter 10.)

"Awake, arise, or be forever fallen!"

—*Milton*

"My vision grew bigger," she told me. "I

went from *someday* I can own my own home to *now* I will own a house, even a brand-new car, and I won't be selfish and greedy. I deserve it."

Then she added, cutting right to the core of all underearning, "It never occurred to me I was limiting myself, defeating my own purpose. When I got that, *something clicked*. My work was worth more because *I was worth more*."

Tami's comments give us a glimpse into how high earners think, with statements like, "my vision grew bigger," "I'll do it *now*," and most of all, "I deserve it." But even more, she hands us the key to breaking our earnings barrier. It's what I call the **Click.**

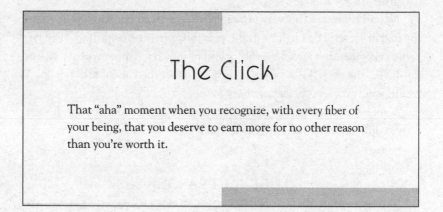

The Click

That "aha" moment when you recognize, with every fiber of your being, that you deserve to earn more for no other reason than you're worth it.

When you finally awaken to your value, you're primed for the next level. But until that click occurs, you might as well be going against gravity.

> "Nothing is more exciting and rewarding than the sudden flash of insight that leaves you a changed person . . ."
>
> —*Arthur Gordon*

THE SEARCH FOR WHAT WORKS

The importance of the Click jumped out at me while I was interviewing people who'd been through my workshops or who'd done the workbook on their own. I discovered that everyone fell into roughly two categories: those who made significant changes and those who didn't. (I call the first group **Doers,** and the other **Dawdlers.**)

Virtually everyone was motivated to change. Almost all reported at least one new insight. Yet for some, nothing happened. They came in underearners, and they stayed underearners. Why?

Because the problem we're dealing with isn't really about money at all. *Money is simply a metaphor.* In fact, the problem isn't even about overcoming underearning. *Underearning is merely a symptom.* Lasting change never occurs by treating the symptom. My belief is that you've kept yourself an underearner for a reason.

Naomi expressed this very principle when I asked her why she thought she had made so little progress in the year following the workshop. "I've become very clear that my relationship with money is a symptom of my lack of self-love," she said. "I need to quit being so concerned about other people's feelings and problems before my own."

Naomi has pinpointed what lies at the root of all underearning. It's the biggest difference between the Doers and the Dawdlers.

THE REAL REASON

"Why do you think this work has had such a ripple effect in your life," I asked each of the Doers. They all came to the same conclusion. They all described having the Click.

"I think it's about self-worth, about finally feeling that I had a lot to offer," Cheri Schell replied after a thoughtful pause.

> "Don't forget to love yourself."
>
> —*Søren Kierkegaard*

Jody Stevenson put it this way: "Somewhere in the workshop I got that money and self-worth were synonymous. Having debt meant I didn't think highly of myself. Managing my money reminds me I am worthy."

Psychotherapist Sue Bates recognized, "I could finally raise my rates because I started to value what I do. This is about what you feel you deserve in the world."

Similarly, real estate agent Donna Weaver discovered, "I was worth more than I was giving myself credit for. I had knowledge that was valuable and I didn't need to downplay that." A month later she sent me an e-mail: "I just deposited a $14,000 paycheck. That's right, fourteen thousand dollars. I made the conscious choice to have a $10,000 a month income and guess what? Here it is and then some."

> "Self-love is not only necessary and good, it is a prerequisite for loving others."
>
> —*Rollo May*

These words fly straight to the heart of the Inner Work, capturing the essence of our economic plight. Bottom line: *Underearning is a condition of low self-esteem.* Inside every underearner lies some degree of hopelessness or helplessness brought on by a perceived lack of self-worth or absence of self-love.

Dave Elvin, an amateur actor, expressed it so well: "I know I need to work on really believing in myself, caring for myself, doing things that build dignity. And from that dignity will come the desire to love myself with meaningful work paying more money."

Self-esteem, success, power, and prosperity are intricately entwined. When you begin valuing yourself, your finances inevitably improve, along with most everything else. Conversely, low self-esteem makes it difficult, if not impossible, to reach the next level. Why? Because you don't believe you can. And there's no better way to reinforce that belief, limit your power, diminish your value, than by lowering your earning potential. It all works together.

> "Self-esteem—the ability to look upon yourself as having value."
>
> —*Dr. John Nemiah,* Foundations of Psychopathology

I vividly remember a psychologist I interviewed who was stunned at what she'd discovered: "I realized the problem was me, the way I was presenting myself to the world. I wasn't taking myself seriously. I never framed my degrees and put them on the wall. It was like 'That doesn't matter.' Well, it does matter. I didn't project a very good image, more like I don't deserve it. I'd find myself apologizing all the time or using self-deprecating humor. I sort of had an inkling I was doing this, but I never understood why."

Now, let's try this exercise.

Self-Esteem Inventory

Check any item that applies to you.

☐ I blame someone else for my situation.

☐ I constantly blame myself even if it's not my fault.

☐ I do what others want even if I don't want to.

☐ I hold myself back, or easily give in to avoid upsetting, hurting, angering, or offending someone.

☐ I let others demean or put me down.

☐ I hold grudges or I'm easily angered.

☐ I'm reluctant to set lofty goals for fear I won't attain them.

☐ I'm filled with big dreams but don't follow through.

☐ I give up at the first sign of failure or hint of rejection.

☐ I'm embarrassed or scared to make mistakes.

☐ I don't do what I say I'm going to do.

☐ I'm unwilling to ask for what I want, often because I don't even know.

☐ I hear myself saying "yes, but" a lot.

☐ I have no control over my time.

☐ I really don't see I have many choices in my life.

If you checked more than two, your self-esteem needs a serious boost. Even one is a red flag. Do you notice how similar these statements are to the characteristics of underearning?

Virtually every six-figure woman I interviewed swore money was not her primary motivation. But at the same time she fully expected to be well compensated because *she knew she was worth it.*

As one of those women, Lois Carrier, told me, "Until a woman learns to value herself, she's not going to be valued by an employer (or client)."

This sums up the purpose of the five steps we're coming to next, and my desired outcome for you in reading this book. Breaking through your barriers requires that Click, the recognition that you *really are* a capable person with something valuable to offer, and you understand beyond doubt—no matter how vehemently those little voices may argue—that you deserve to be happy, successful, and well paid *because you're worth it.*

In fact, this even explains why so many women I interviewed lost weight. Believe me, I never expected this. When I asked Dr. Christiane Northrup, author of *Women's Bodies, Women's Wisdom*, about this finding, however, she wasn't surprised at all. She explained that it's a logical progression from recognizing your value to shedding those extra pounds because you're feeling fulfilled, more empowered, and thus motivated to take better care of yourself.

"The reason is this," Dr. Northrup wrote me in an e-mail, "earning more money is associated with an enhanced sense of personal power and self-esteem. Women who take on more than their share of responsibility often carry too much weight. And many take on this responsibility because they don't feel good about themselves. So the habit of service to others and neglect of self becomes a default setting.

"But once self-esteem is enhanced through asking for more money—and more of the good that life has to offer—women find themselves so fulfilled that they don't need to fill the emptiness with food or other addictions."

> "[Self-esteem is] the experience of being capable of meeting life's challenges and being worthy of happiness."
>
> —*National Association for Self-Esteem*

> "Self-esteem—warm personal regard from within."
>
> —*Pia Mellody, internationally recognized authority on addiction, author of* **Facing Codependence**

THE ART AND SCIENCE OF HIGH SELF-ESTEEM

In the end, overcoming underearning is an act of individuation—a psychological term referring to the developmental phase when a child separates from her parents. Individuation insists that you not only break free from other's expectations to become your own person, but that you value who you are enough to put your own needs at the top of your list. As Charles Schwab, the wealthy industrialist, warned us a century ago, "The man who tries to please everyone, ends up whittling himself away."

This, however, is what women, in particular, have been doing for generations—paring ourselves down by putting everyone else first. It's the way many of us were raised. To do otherwise feels selfish. But as my colleague Marcia Brixey always says, **"Selfish** is when you're not doing what someone else wants you to do." Our unwillingness to respect our needs, to give priority to our dreams, because it feels selfish and wrong, explains why so many continue to underearn.

THE MOST IMPORTANT
FINANCIAL ADVICE YOU'LL EVER GET

Every time you go to do something different, every time you deviate from the norm, every time you break a habit or end a pattern, your brain cries, "Stop, this doesn't feel right! Don't do it."

DO NOT LISTEN.

The number one requirement for financial success (or success in anything for that matter) is simply this: *You've got to be willing to be uncomfortable.* Or as Eastern wisdom advocates, "Embrace what does not come naturally. Only then will you stop limiting yourself."

Discomfort is an automatic response to anything out of the ordinary. The ability to tolerate discomfort is absolutely essential to go to the next level in any area of your life. Anxiety, fear, worry, nervousness, resistance . . . all these are normal reactions to new situations. *It need not mean something's wrong. It just means that something is different.* Or as my wonderful therapist, Rosalie Thomas, would say to me, "Recognize you're tapping into the challenge of change."

The challenge of change almost always elicits the same response. "This is soooo hard." I hear it all the time in the workshops as we discuss the steps and what we need to do. I call it the **Underearner Whine.** My response never varies. "This is *not* hard. It's easy. But it *is* uncomfortable."

> "We've been programmed to sacrifice everything in the name of what is good and right for everyone else. I know for sure you can't give what you don't have."
>
> —*Oprah Winfrey*

"I really liked how you kept saying, 'you are going to be uncomfortable,'" Sally Beckett told me. "I now see that fear is an indicator, not of something to avoid, but something to approach. I don't think as adults we can experience true change without some form of fear, pain, or discomfort. Because if it was easy to change, we all would have done it."

Actually, Sally, it *is* easy. It's just not comfortable.

TOUGH STUFF

The Inner Work takes courage. "After the workshop there was a period of very hard growth," Sally told me. "I needed to understand why I was where I was and get clear about the internal messages that I absorbed as a child, and throughout my life, that were leading to the types of decisions I was making now. I had never looked at those messages before."

She paused, then admitted, "The excavation hurt, but I knew I wasn't going to heal unless I brought it all out."

If the Inner Work is tough for women, it can be even more challenging for men.

"I'm a guy. I don't like to think about what

> Fred Sanford, to his son, Lamont: "Didn't you ever learn anything from being my son? Who do you think I'm doing this all for?"
>
> Lamont: "Yourself."
>
> Fred smiles: "Yeah, you learned something."
>
> —*From* Sanford and Son, *a popular sitcom from the 1970s*

is going on in my head," conceded her husband, Jason Beckett. "I had a lot of resistance to examining myself. My resistance showed up as 'I'm too tired to deal with this now.' " He laughed, admitting that the excuse was so transparent, he couldn't help but see right through it.

"As an artist, the message I got was I would never be successful. It took quite a change to go from being 'the kid who is just a dreamer' to 'the guy who owns and operates an extremely successful business.' What I had to do was get out of that internal conflict."

It was also embarrassing. "I have this thing that I should know how to do everything I need to do. That's how I was raised. But how are you ever going to learn anything if your first reaction is embarrassment about what you don't know, and you run away from it?"

What kept you with it? I asked.

"I had to want the result badly enough to put up with it. I had to focus on what I was going to gain. It got painful enough to say, 'I am not willing to stay in this place anymore, so in spite of the pain, which I realize is all about avoidance, I am going to do this work because it hurts too much not to.' "

> **"The only thing money gives you is the freedom not to worry about money."**
> —*Johnny Carson*

It's when you make that same crucial commitment—wanting the results badly enough to do the work—that you open the door to be amply rewarded.

THE "WHYS" AND "WHY NOTS"

Let's start the Inner Work with two very basic exercises. First, ask yourself these questions: *Why do I want to increase my income? What would I have in my life that I don't have now?*

It's important to identify your motivation. You're more apt to change when you believe what you're learning has value.

For most people, the reasons have to do with financial security and living their dreams. Here are some examples from the workshop.

★ I want a better life for my kids.
★ I want to help my mother.
★ I just got divorced.
★ I'm sick of struggle.
★ I know I'm worth more.

★ I'm scared what will happen if I don't.
★ I long to visit Tahiti.
★ I always wanted to create a foundation.
★ I worry about retirement.

Write your reasons below.

I Want to Increase My Income Because . . .

Next, finish the following sentence with your first reaction.

I'd Love to Make More Money, *But* . . .

Some examples of how others have responded:

★ I have little kids.
★ I'm scared.
★ I never went to college.
★ I don't have time.

★ I'm too old.
★ I'm too young.
★ I don't know how.

Your response to this statement reveals the assumptions and beliefs you hold about what you need to do, need to be, or need to have to make more money. Only the last response, "I don't know how," is a valid one. That's why you're reading this book. Few of us have been taught the five simple steps to overcoming underearning.

Instead, we have conjured up all kinds of reasons why we can't do it. I was as guilty as anyone. But as I learned from my interviews with six-figure women, everything I thought it took to make big money was wrong. I met women who

- ✓ didn't even have a seventh-grade education.
- ✓ worked in jobs you'd never expect to be high paying.
- ✓ were working far fewer hours than most underearners.
- ✓ didn't start making big bucks until they were in their fifties, sixties, even seventies.
- ✓ were riddled with fear and self-doubt.

The point is, every single one of our "reasons," as convincing as they may seem, are nothing more than fabrications, flimsy excuses issuing from fear, not fact. For every excuse you give me, I'll show you someone in the same boat who is prospering.

A TASTE OF WHAT'S
TO COME—REAL-LIFE EXAMPLES

I've chosen two women we've already met who are definitely Doers, who did a great job of combining the Inner and Outer Work. Their stories illustrate how to use this book for optimal success. Just in case you miss something, I've listed "Eight Rules for Achieving Remarkable Results" near the end of this chapter.

CHERI'S STORY

"There's a tendency when you do a workshop like this to get excited and start doing stuff and then things kind of creep back in," Cheri Schell told me. "I could slip back so easily." But she never did, at least not for long.

Cheri was the massage therapist we met in the first chapter who not only upped her income, but went down several dress sizes. You'd never guess she was over fifty, with her freckled face and thick mane of chestnut hair.

She came to the workshop "feeling a lot of despair" and left saying, "I can do this." What did that mean? I asked her.

"I used to beat myself up for doing such a bad job handling my finances, getting into debt. After the workshop, I said, 'Okay, this is what you've done. Now what can you start doing differently?' " She realized, "I had to stop blaming my mother's negligence with her money for my own situation. It was time to move on. I had to start taking control."

Before the workshop, she said, "I would come to work an hour before church on Sunday, go without lunch, start at 6 a.m. if that's what people wanted, because I was afraid they'd go to somebody else. I was accepting insurance to satisfy my clients, but it paid less than my normal hourly rate, the paperwork was astronomical, and it was a constant battle just to get paid."

Then, during the class, she saw the light. "I realized that most of my life I did what people wanted me to do. I wanted to be liked. I wanted to be seen as somebody nice." She didn't think "nice" people said no, raised their rates, or refused insurance.

"All that changed," she said, "when I started putting a value on my time and my talents. I knew I had to take care of me first."

She stopped accommodating everyone else and started setting boundaries for herself. She closed insurance contracts, accepted only cash, raised her rates $10, shortened her one-hour sessions to fifty minutes, said no to people who couldn't pay, and blocked out time for herself.

"I had to start turning people down. That was really hard. I felt like a jerk," Cheri said, referring to the discomfort of saying no to someone in physical pain. Though she didn't lose a single client despite extensive changes, she readily admits it's been difficult to stay on track. "Just the other day, I caught myself overscheduling, booking too many appointments, and had to go back, call the people, and reschedule."

How did she keep herself going?

"I do something every day," she explained. "I have my workbook with me pretty much wherever I go. Every morning, over coffee, I read something.

"Whenever that voice comes up and says, 'You're only a massage therapist,' I look at why it's not true. Why my town is a good market, why I'm good at what I do, and why my services are valuable."

The result? She's had time to go to Weight Watchers, fix healthy meals, create downtime for herself, and still make more money. Right after the interview, she told me, she was taking a week off to go to a spa. No wonder she was feeling so much better about herself.

SALLY'S STORY

I first met Sally Beckett when she came to my home to interview me for a local magazine. Clad in colorful prints and flowing fabric, she reminded me of a fortysomething pixie. At the time she was deeply in debt, earning minimum wage in a variety of odd jobs, freelancing for magazines, writing novels, and working in a gift shop. I invited her to one of my early workshops.

In less than a year, Sally reduced her debt significantly, created a $12,000 nest egg from scratch, launched a business with her husband, signed a multiple-book contract for a minimum of $35,000, and began teaching writing workshops.

"I came home from the class very serious about making changes," Sally recalled. "I was like a bull that keeps her head down and keeps plowing through. It's the difference between someone *considering* change and someone *committing* to change.

"I saw my patterns, issues I'd been avoiding, and by seeing them, I could change them." She then started asking herself, "How can I make changes and have fun doing it?"

She knew the first step was to respect her own needs to improve her finances and focus exclusively on writing books. She sat down with her husband and explained what she was doing. "He had to get on board with me. One can't grow and the other stay static. We got very clear on what changes we needed to make. Then we found small ways to make these changes. Like we'd go out to dinner, split a meal, and bank the savings."

In the meantime, Sally left her day job to commit full-time to writing. "It was very hard to do, but I had to walk out on a limb." As often happens, fate intervened. "Literally the day I left, an editor called saying she was buying my book."

Soon after the workshop, Sally's house, which had been on the market three years, unexpectedly sold. The reason: instead of relying on her husband to handle it, she took the reins. "The house had been such a financial drain," she said. So she called the realtor and issued an ultimatum—if the house didn't sell soon, she'd find another agent. Her agent complied.

Suddenly, she had three weeks to find another home. It was a "huge" task, consuming all her time. But instead of putting her finances on the back burner, she applied the concepts she had learned to the move itself.

"I kept them in the forefront of my mind. I used the move as an opportunity to learn, change my patterns, to ask for what I need.

"I still find it easy to get back into struggle," Sally admitted. But keeping a journal has helped her immensely. "I keep writing in my workbook so I can refer back to it, see my progress. Now when I feel frustrated, I'll go back and say, 'Okay, three months ago I felt dumb and stuck because I didn't know where my money was,' and now I'm way past that. Now I'm learning to accept and live with all the abundance that I've been experiencing."

THE DOERS VERSUS THE DAWDLERS

Both Sally and Cheri, and all the other Doers, consistently displayed certain behaviors that were absent from stories told by the Dawdlers.

If you genuinely want to be a financial success, if you're truly ready to go to the next level in your life, it's a no brainer. Follow what the Doers do. Here's how.

Eight Rules for Achieving Remarkable Results

1. **Make a vow to yourself: underearning is no longer an option.** One woman put it this way: "There has to be a place you get to where there are no back doors." Take the exercises seriously. Spend time reflecting on your responses. Write in your journal regularly. (Dawdlers may swear they want to change, but they ignore or downplay the work, and don't do anything different.)

2. **Keep your commitments.** Do what you say you're going to do. As a young man pointed out, "If something is important and you

don't follow through, it chips away at your self-esteem. I feel like now I trust I'll do what I say I'm going to do, like paying off the debt." (Dawdlers often fail to keep promises, especially to themselves.)

3. **Use disruptions (like moving or getting married) to practice the five steps.** Incorporate what you learn about earning into whatever situations arise. (Dawdlers let life get in the way, becoming easily derailed by even the smallest distractions.)

4. **Enroll your spouse or significant other in this process.** This often involves some degree of confrontation. (Dawdlers avoid conflict at all cost.)

5. **Put yourself first.** Call it *the message of the oxygen mask:* if you don't take care of yourself, you're in no shape to care for anyone else. (Dawdlers deplete themselves for the sake of others.)

6. **Keep passages from this book, or snippets of inspiration, where you can easily see them.** Put quotes or lists (like this one) on the refrigerator or in your wallet, taped to a mirror, even hanging in a gym locker. Revisit the book often. (How Dawdlers do it: out of sight, out of mind.)

7. **Rigorously observe your actions and thoughts.** Deliberately shift when you catch yourself exhibiting underearning traits or self-sabotaging behavior. (Dawdlers are experts at justifying, rationalizing, and making excuses.)

8. **Do what you dread.** If there's something you don't want to do, that's precisely what you must do first. The more frightening or daunting it seems, the more important it is to face. (Dawdlers go to great lengths to avoid the unpleasant, fearful, or uncomfortable.)

If you're ready to take responsibility, you've arrived at the starting gate. In the next section, we'll be going through each of the five steps that can make a Doer out of you. It will help immensely to keep these rules in front of you each step of the way. Now, let the F.U.N!* begin!

CHAPTER THREE HIGHLIGHTS

★ High earners think differently than underearners. Consequently, they make different choices and produce different results.

★ To break through your earning barriers you need to shift your thinking, combining the Inner with the Outer Work, to arrive at the Click, that "aha" moment when you recognize your value.

★ The number one requirement to overcome underearning and raise self-esteem is the *willingness to be uncomfortable*.

★ To get the most from this book, follow the Doers:

1. Make a vow: underearning is no longer an option.
2. Keep your commitments.
3. Use disruptions to practice the five steps.
4. Enroll your spouse or significant other in the process.
5. Put yourself first.
6. Keep passages from this book where you can see them.
7. Rigorously observe your actions and thoughts.
8. Do what you dread.

---

* Financial Understanding Now! Yes, this can actually be fun. Ask the women in my workshop. Better yet, see for yourself!

Conversation with Myself

Which rule(s) on the list might be particularly difficult for you? Were there any surprises? What can you do to remind yourself to follow these rules? On a 1 to 10 scale, how would you rate your self-esteem? If it's low, do you know why? How do you feel about doing the Inner Work?

Taking the Steps

"*The moment you move out of your own way, you make room for miracles to occur.*"

—Dr. Barbara King

"*Si se puede.*"
[*Yes, it's possible.*]

—*What Cesar Chavez challenged farmworkers to say when they didn't know how to overcome challenges*

FOUR

Step 1:
Tell the Truth

*"A matter that becomes clear
ceases to concern us."*

—*Nietzsche*

TURN ON THE LIGHT

While writing this chapter, a decades-old memory kept flashing to mind, like blinking neon begging for attention. It didn't take me long to figure out why.

I am sitting in the office of Karen McCall, a gifted counselor and pioneer in recovery from chronic debting, overspending, and underearning. She has patiently listened to my horror stories of an unscrupulous husband, humongous tax bills, and my hopeless stupidity with money. Her eyes fix on mine, a long pause ensues, then she speaks with a firmness I'll never forget.

"You've got to get out of the dark," she insists, "or nothing I say will help you at all."

Looking back, I recognize this was my introduction to the important first step. Coming out of the dark meant I had to tell myself the truth. I had to literally turn on the light and start looking at all the stuff I'd been artfully

"The truth is the only safe ground to stand on."

—*Elizabeth Cady Stanton*

dodging or inadvertently denying. I had no idea at the time the extraordinary impact this one small step would have on my financial future.

In the following weeks, I began going through all kinds of papers, tracking my spending, organizing my records, figuring out what I had, understanding where my money was.

Believe me, this wasn't accomplished without a fierce internal battle. I'd procrastinate until the night before my weekly visits to Karen. Sometimes I'd walk into her office with nothing but excuses. Eventually, however, the piles of scattered paper found their way into neatly marked files. As my desk became clearer, so did my thinking. I could feel the fog in my brain literally lifting.

At the same time, she had me writing a money autobiography (see the following Journal Exercise, "Money Autobiography"), responding to questions about my personal history. Exploring my feelings was as eye opening as examining my finances, maybe even more so. I discovered why I'd made certain choices, and in most cases, I didn't like what I saw. I had been living a script I didn't write, a script that told me, among other things, managing money is a man's job. Until then, it never even dawned on me to think any differently. Figuring this out freed me to make changes. For the very first time, I started to feel some semblance of control, not only over my money, but my whole life as well.

HOW IT WORKS

Telling the truth is a prerequisite for higher pay. Without it, to paraphrase Karen, nothing I write, or anyone else says, will help you at all. What's more, finding the truth lays the foundation for the four steps that follow.

Telling the truth involves both the Outer Work (getting crystal clear about your cash flow) and the Inner Work (figuring out your emotional blocks and internal motivation). The exercises throughout this book are specifically designed to help you do this.

If the idea of scrutinizing your life causes a sudden spike in your anxiety level, relax. We're going to take it slow. All that's required at this point is

Journal Exercise

MONEY AUTOBIOGRAPHY

These questions are adapted from "Your Money Autobiography" in the *Financial Recovery Workbook*, by Karen McCall. Spend some time writing the answers in your journal.

What were your early memories of money?

Were you given an allowance growing up?

Were you paid for chores or grades?

What was your experience being paid (or not being paid)?

How old were you when you first started to earn money?

What did you do?

How did you feel?

What's the most you've ever made? The least?

How was money handled in your family?

What messages were you given about work and money?

Was there any emotional trauma around money?

What was your biggest fear about money when you were younger?

What were your parents' fears?

---

that you complete the four exercises in *this* chapter as honestly as you can. Step 1 is intended as an act of admission, nothing more.

That said, there's tremendous power in telling the truth. Clarity alone often generates change. The simple act of admitting what's not working and analyzing why has been known to spontaneously motivate people to take action. When you combine financial clarity with personal insight, a powerful alchemy occurs. Counterproductive habits give way to enlightened choices. "When you get clear, the way opens," one woman said. Or as another put it, "It's a key to another universe."

I witnessed this in my own life. I saw it repeatedly with others. I immediately think of Marvella McPartland, a plump, auburn-haired grandmother who was sixty-five when she came to my workshop in Portland, Oregon.

Marvella was a classic underearner who spent her adult life trying not to be one. Even in the 1960s, when she had a recording contract with a major studio and saw two of her records shoot up the charts, she had very little money to show for it. Today, she works three jobs—as a music minister in a church, an actress, and a picture framer—but up until recently, she's always struggled to make ends meet.

Last year, however, her financial life dramatically shifted. "Since the workshop, I've had a steady increase in my income," she told me proudly. "I was at poverty level. Last year I grossed $50,000. This year it's going to be even more."

Doing the exercises opened her eyes, she said. "When you had us looking at our childhood, all the ways we've been programmed, I realized I had a lot of negative conditioning to unravel. I had to get out of my massive self-judgment and negativity."

Never before had she connected the dots, linking past experience to her present predicament. "My father, a Swedish immigrant, called me a 'shit kid' in Swedish twenty times a day," she recalled. "And my mother told me it was bad to be materialistic, and selfish to want more. In recalling this negative input, I realized I'd set my standards way too low.

"No wonder I wasn't able to capitalize on my early success (as a singer). I wasn't programmed. I shot myself in the foot."

I asked how she did that.

"I was the kind of person who would write checks and pray there'd be enough money to cover them," she explained.

Coming out of denial is what changed things. "I didn't do anything differently other than keep better track of where I was and know that I truly deserved to succeed," Marvella said. She started balancing her checkbook, put little bits aside in savings, and watched her income almost miraculously grow.

"I had gone to all these prosperity workshops and nothing happened, nothing changed," she said. "Now I realize it's a knuckling-down process, like unraveling a ball of yarn. I have to know what's going on. If I don't know, then I can't create anything differently."

UNRAVELING YOUR OWN TANGLED WEB

Until you really know what's going on, you can't possibly do anything differently. Unless you confess what's not working and figure out why, you'll never be able to make things work any better.

A crucial piece of this process is to accept that for the most part your life is a result of the choices you've made. But many of those choices have been based on false, deficient, or flawed information. Think about all the financial details you haven't wanted to deal with, or how Blanche's negative chatter drowns out your authentic needs and desires. Choices derived from this kind of data aren't likely to lead you in the direction of your dreams. The whole point of telling the truth is to start making new choices based on actual fact (not your stories about what happened), accurate data (not what you guess is going on), and your core values (not what you *should* want).

> "I didn't lose myself all at once. I rubbed out my face over the years. The same way carvings on stone are worn down by water."
>
> —*Amy Tan*

THE OUTER WORK IS YOUR STARTING POINT

The best way to begin the first step is by looking a tangible problem (see the checklist on page 77) square in the face instead of sweeping it under the rug.

Financial achievement is always preceded by a financial challenge. Your particular challenge could be as subtle as a sneaky suspicion that something's not right, or as obvious as the agonizing awareness that you can't pay your rent. Underearners' willingness to tackle a problem, whatever it was, personal or financial, turned out to be a pivotal step in their journey to success.

Problems have a purpose. They're trying to get our attention. They let us know we need to do something differently. It's always best to

> "The only thing I have to release in order to get what I want is my story about why I can't have it."
>
> —*Source unknown*

deal with them early before they become any bigger. Troubles usually begin as a whisper, but grow progressively louder the longer we neglect them.

Facing a problem does not mean rushing ahead with an impulsive solution or passively accepting the situation, as *That's just the way it is."*

Facing a problem means looking it straight in the eye, even if you haven't a clue what to do about it. "The truth I had to tell myself was that I'd been ignoring my finances," Laurie Lamoureux, a former paralegal, now a brand-new business owner, told me. "I knew we were living month to month. I knew we had debts. But I didn't know how much."

Your first peek at the truth may evoke temporary panic. But then something remarkable will occur, as you'll soon learn from Laurie's story. Situations can rapidly improve when you finally remove the blindfold.

EXERCISE: PINPOINTING THE PROBLEMS, PART I

Let's begin the Outer Work. Here's a two-part exercise to help you pull back the curtain and start identifying what's not working in your life. Read the Problem Indicator Checklist on page 77, then mark any statements that ring true for you.

EXERCISE: PINPOINTING THE PROBLEMS, PART II

Next, go back and look at your responses to the Underearning Quiz on page 25. Referring to that quiz and the statements you just checked, fill in the box on page 78. Write down any challenges, large or small, that are staring you in the face or hovering somewhere on the horizon. Remember, this is not about fixing them. The idea is to pinpoint those areas that need some attention.

Problem Indicator Checklist

Check the statements that apply to you.

- ☐ Deep down, I believe someone/something will rescue me.
- ☐ Someone else handles all my financial decisions.
- ☐ I rarely balance my checkbook.
- ☐ I forget to record checks I've written.
- ☐ I don't know the total amount of my debt.
- ☐ Creditors keep calling me.
- ☐ I use credit cards for cash advances at the ATM.
- ☐ I don't have a savings account.
- ☐ I only pay the minimum monthly credit card payment.
- ☐ I can't even afford monthly payments.
- ☐ I was recently turned down for credit or a loan.
- ☐ I have less than two months' living expenses in the bank.
- ☐ I routinely spend more than I earn.
- ☐ If I lost my job, I'd have difficulty paying the next month's bills.
- ☐ I don't know my net worth.
- ☐ I worry about money a lot.
- ☐ I have trouble paying my rent or house payments on time.
- ☐ I put off seeking medical attention because I can't afford it.
- ☐ I dip into savings and investments to pay bills.
- ☐ I take out new loans before my old ones are paid off.
- ☐ I have back taxes I've never paid.

The statements you checked are your "troublemakers." If they're not causing you problems yet, they eventually will.

What's Not Working in My Life

Don't be surprised if you're inclined to skip this exercise, telling yourself you'll get back to it later. Avoidance, which is common to underearning, becomes a habit. Now's the time to start breaking it. Exposing the truth *is* uncomfortable. When we turn on the light, we rarely like what we see, which is why we've been avoiding it in the first place. Please don't skip this exercise. Fill in the box above before you go any farther. As Chinese physician Hans Huuyin tells us, "Truth like surgery may hurt, but it cures."

SEEING THE LIGHT

I talked to Laurie Lamoureux barely a month after she took my workshop.

"I haven't hit six figures yet, but I have a lot more motivation to look at things I've been avoiding," she told me. "It was really hard to do. I had to make myself look at everything and how I got here."

The first thing she did, after the class, was add up what she and her husband owed. The grand total was a whopping $40,000.

"Did you know your debt would be so high?" I asked.

"I did but I didn't. I think there's a part of your brain that just doesn't want to think about the total numbers. I knew everything individually but when you have it spread out . . ." Her voice trailed off, then she sighed. "It doesn't feel good to admit that if we don't do something soon, we're going to be eating cat food when we're sixty-five."

> "We can easily forgive a child who is afraid of the dark. The real tragedy is when adults are afraid of the light."
>
> —*Unknown source*

Telling a truth you've been trying to hide is like going from pitch black into blinding light. It's shocking at first, perhaps even painful, and your instinctive reaction is to keep your eyes closed.

Later, Laurie told me, "I wrote in my journal, 'Am I willing to be even more uncomfortable than I am now for a while?' And I underlined 'for a while.' I remembered how you kept coming back to 'you are going to be uncomfortable.' It validated my discomfort, and I'll probably continue to be uncomfortable while I'm fixing this. If I hadn't been aware of that, I think it would've stopped me."

Instead, she stopped taking on new debt, consolidated her cards to the lowest possible rate, began seeing a financial counselor to learn better money management skills, and started selling on eBay "a lot of stuff that's just sitting around taking up space" like books, videos, and craft items. She also rented a space at an antique mall to sell "small collectibles that we have way too many of. Having too much stuff is another bad way to manage money."

> "It's not looking that makes us afraid."
>
> —*Unknown source*

What she discovered was priceless. "I won't tell anyone it's easy looking at what you've been avoiding forever. It's really hard. But it won't kill you. And you know, it wasn't as bad as I thought. It actually feels a lot better than saying, 'I don't want to look at it.' "

The courage it took for Laurie to look truth in the eye gave an unexpected boost to her business, unpacking new homeowners. "It's motivated me to make extra calls, schedule extra appointments. It's pushed me past my comfort threshold to do a little bit more than I had been doing to get the word out."

DIGGING DOWN TO THE ROOTS

The Outer Work, of course, only deals with what we can see, and there's always more to underearning than meets the eye. Telling the truth is like digging up dandelions. If you don't get down to the roots, all your hard work will be for nothing. Down among the roots is where the Inner Work occurs.

Sometimes the roots are surprisingly small, shallow, easy to pull. Other times, they're so deeply buried, it takes more exertion to get to the bottom. Getting to the truth can be a complex process that may not happen right away. I'm giving you some fabulous tools, in the form of exercises, I've been using for years. But they require concerted effort and concentrated thought on your part. I promise you, it'll be worth the effort when you can say to yourself, "Oh, so that's why I've been making these choices." At that moment, you're finally free to make new choices. Finding the truth also means getting rid of the lies.

> **"The revolution begins within."**
>
> *—Gloria Steinem*

"I saw something I never thought of before," said Ginger Moshofsky, explaining the growth spurt in her network marketing business. "I had never connected the hardship from my childhood to what is happening with me today. I really thought I had a great childhood. I just pushed anything else aside, thinking, 'Is it really helpful to dwell on the past?' I still believe you don't necessarily have to dwell, but what I didn't realize is that my past was creating a filter and a paradigm for how I saw myself and the world." Ginger knew she had an aversion to taking risks. The truth was she really feared being scolded or ridiculed, as she'd been as a child but had completely blocked out.

People rarely respond to a situation directly, only to their interpretation of it based on prior programming. The next exercise on page 82 will help you explore your early conditioning and understand how your conclusions have limited your reach—as if they had you on a leash.

Laurie explained what she discovered. "My biggest fear around money is that I won't have any when I *retire*. And that even if I did have more income, somehow it still wouldn't be enough. This was a huge awakening. I suddenly realized I *won't* have more money until I prove I can take care of what I have."

Sally Beckett was also surprised at what this exercise revealed. "My mother always said, 'It's better to struggle financially because once your husband has money, he's going to leave.' Without realizing it, I have this wonderful twenty-year marriage that's full of financial struggle. I accepted those messages without ever examining them. I realized it doesn't have to be this way."

No matter how illogical or silly an insight may seem, as long as it's hidden, we're helpless. Awareness alone gives us access to new choices.

"I never realized until I did the sentence completion exercise, how afraid I was that if I became rich, I'd give all my money to my daughter," one woman confessed, almost sheepishly. "It made me wake up to the fact I've got to set boundaries."

Similarly another admitted, "The truth I had to tell myself was I used food and debt to numb my pain. If I wasn't feeling good, I'd buy something to feel better. Or I'd eat. I'm not going to do that anymore. I got very focused. I sat down and wrote a plan for how much money I was going to put toward paying off my Visa bill. I'm completely out of debt now, and I've opened up a savings account. I only buy things I can afford."

Of course, not all past programming is negative. For instance, gallery owner Debra Van Tuinen realized her frivolous spending was not part of her upbringing. "That's not the way I was raised. But I felt since my husband was doing it, I deserved to do it, too. I never got that before. But it's so obvious to me now!"

Exercise: Digging Down to the Roots

Complete the following sentences with the first words that come to mind. Don't censure what you get or look for the "right" answer. Let yourself go with your very first reaction. And do it quickly. You can always change your responses later.

1. My biggest fear about money is

2. My father felt money was

3. My mother felt money was

4. In my family, money caused

5. My early experience with money was

6. Money equals

7. I'm afraid if I had more money, I would

8. In order to have more money, I'd need to

9. When I have money, I usually

10. If I could afford it, I would

11. People with money are

12. I'd have more money if

What did you learn?

How did your early experiences and parental messages affect you?

What would you like to change?

Discuss your responses with at least one other person. Continue to mull them over for the next few days and see what comes up for you.

Journal Exercise

Complete the following sentence with the first word that comes to your mind. Do it at least fifteen times. Write your responses quickly, without thinking.

Money is _____.   Money is _____.   Money is _____.

Money is _____.   Money is _____.   Money is _____.

Money is _____.   Money is _____.   Money is _____.

Money is _____.   Money is _____.   Money is _____.

Money is _____.   Money is _____.   Money is _____.

Write in your journal about your experience doing this.

EYES WIDE OPEN

Remember Odette, the entrepreneur who wasn't paying herself adequately and wondered if she was actually an underearner? She was initially skeptical about doing the Inner Work.

"I never wanted to blame my childhood. For me, that's a cop out. Come on, it's over. But it does matter if you are unconscious," she exclaimed. "I had forgotten my roots. How it influenced the way I think. I just blocked it all out.

"I had forgotten how money always caused a lot of tension in my family. My parents were poor so we lived in my aunt's bakery complex. We grew up in this fancy compound, but it wasn't ours, it was my aunt's. I have this thing in the back of my head: it doesn't matter what you see around you. None of it's yours.

> "When one is pretending the entire body revolts."
>
> —Anaïs Nin

"In high school, I worked my butt off, and maybe if I was lucky, I'd get a dollar or two, or maybe my aunt would take me to McDonald's."

THE BIG LIE

Odette discovered what Oliver Wendell Holmes told us long ago, "All limitations are self-imposed." To believe otherwise is the **Big Lie,** an extraordinary self-deception where we convince ourselves we are powerless.

"In the workshop, I thought, 'Who's not paying me now, who took my aunt's place?' Me. Wait, I don't have to do this! I saw I was living a lie. I've been basing my whole self-image on unworthiness from years of unpaid labor. I've lived like that's the truth. And it makes me so mad."

It's been said that the truth will set you free, yet as I've witnessed, it may first make you furious. But rather than hold onto her anger, Odette "turned off all the lies," and silently swore, "I'm going to live my truth from now on."

Odette's experience represents the ultimate aim of doing the first step. She discovered what resides within all of us, buried beneath layers of prior programming like a precious artifact waiting to be unearthed—the **Defining Truth,** the key to our power. And it goes like this.

The Defining Truth

No one is doing this to me. I am doing it to myself. Therefore, I have the ability to change it.

The moment we declare for ourselves the Defining Truth, life as we know it will never be the same. You move from being a victim to owning your power. Your Authentic Voice will begin to emerge louder, more clearly than ever before. But don't expect Blanche, the voice of disapproval, to go away without a fight. Discovering your Big Lie is generally followed by a period of doubt and uncertainty, when you're not quite sure what to believe.

The best strategy at this point is just to sit with the uncertainty, endure the discomfort, remind yourself it's temporary—and do this final exercise.

EXERCISE: REPLACING BELIEFS

In the first column, make a list of everything you believe about yourself and money. Put down whatever comes to mind. You can always erase or keep adding more later.

Now, in the second column, next to each belief, write a new one you'd like to replace the old belief with. You may have some positive ones you want to keep. Great. But if the belief is getting in your way, or causing you pain, find one that feels better. Write it down.

Column I	Column II
WHAT I BELIEVE ABOUT MYSELF & MONEY	WHAT I CHOOSE TO BELIEVE
Making money is greedy.	I am earning more money because I'm worth it.

Then, for the next month, repeat to yourself each of those statements in column two at least twice a day, when you first wake up and right before you fall asleep. Write them on index cards and keep them in view. **Affirmations,** positive statements consistently repeated, are surprisingly powerful in programming your subconscious. After all, that's how you were programmed in the first place. Now it's time to reprogram those beliefs you don't want. Whenever you hear something over and over again, even if it's coming from you, you'll actually begin to believe it.

> "The words I am are the two most powerful words in the language. The subconscious takes any sentence that starts with the words I am and interprets it as a command, a directive to make it happen."
>
> —*Jack Canfield about creating effective affirmations, from his book* The Success Principles

CHAPTER FOUR HIGHLIGHTS

★ The first step to overcoming underearning—**telling the truth**—means being honest about your financial situation and exploring your beliefs and attitudes around money.

★ The place to start is by identifying tangible problems, facing them head on, even when there's no solution in sight.

★ You also need to do the Inner Work, figuring out how your early programming and limiting beliefs have restricted your earning potential.

★ You may get angry at your past choices, and doubt your ability to change, but eventually you'll realize how much power you have to create the life you deserve.

Conversation with Myself

What are the lies I've been telling myself? What are the problems I'm facing? What am I willing to do about them? How has my early programming affected my current relationship with money? What beliefs am I ready to change?

"Lift the masks, remove the armor, and let yourself become all that you imagined."

—*Flavia*

FIVE

Step 2:
Make a Decision

*"You don't have a problem to solve,
you have a decision to make."*

—*Robert Schuller*

HAVE YOU MADE UP YOUR MIND?

Not one of us will ever make more money until we explicitly decide that's what we want to do. I saw this with every six-figure woman I spoke to. Her journey to success began the second she stated, with utter conviction: "It's time to make more money." The exact same can be said for men as well.

A decision is not the same as a wish, a dream, or even the goal you set for yourself in an earlier chapter. Certainly, those are the precursors. But where *a goal denotes the desired destination, a decision implies the determination to reach it.* A decision is a promise you make to yourself, a declaration of intention, that says you're willing to walk through fire to make it happen.

I remember the very day I made my decision. I took out a yellow Post-it note and wrote down a number that just popped into my head—$125,000. That was how much I was going to make that year. I stuck the Post-it on my computer, then took out my journal.

"Is this a fantasy to say I want to make $125,000? How can I? Last year I didn't even make enough to fund an IRA. Do I have what it takes? I honestly don't know. On one hand it seems so possible, especially after talking to all these six-figure women. But another part is saying, 'Oh sure, dream on! Who the hell are you to think you could ever operate on that level?' Deep down, I truly believe if I do the Inner Work, the tide will turn. But it may take a miracle!"

Days later, my second (now ex-) husband walked into my office, glanced at the Post-it note, and asked me what it meant. When I told him, he burst out laughing. I started laughing, too. It *was* ridiculous. But as soon as he left, I tore off the note, added in bold letters, "YES I CAN!" and stuck it right back on my computer. That evening, I reaffirmed my declaration in my journal:

"I'm going to do it! I don't know how, but I know I will. I feel like when that knowingness kicks in, success is assured. (Of course, I'll only be able to prove that in hindsight.)"

By the end of the year I had made six figures. I just wish I hadn't waited so long to make the decision to do it.

DO YOU HAVE A PROFIT MOTIVE?

Making a decision means slamming shut all the doors to other options, blocking off the exits, and, no matter what happens, keep moving toward your destination because anything else is unacceptable.

Here's the beauty of this step. All you have to do is decide what you want and do what comes next (we'll get to the "doing" in the third step). You don't need a plan all figured out, or even believe that it's possible.

The single requirement is a conscious commitment that making more money is a top priority—what's otherwise known as a **profit motive.**

This isn't the way underearners are used to thinking. "It's an embarrassing thing to say you want to make money," one woman admitted demurely. "You're supposed to do good things for other people without being concerned about a reward for yourself. My dad is like that, and it somehow transferred over to me."

> "Not planning has permitted me to accept all the twists and turns [in my career]."
>
> —*Condoleezza Rice*

It may never occur to an underearner to make money a priority. I'll never forget the expression on one woman's face when she exclaimed: "I'm marveling that it's okay to be interested in money."

It's not just okay, it's obligatory. What if your doctor diagnosed you as having a deteriorating condition that could seriously affect the quality of your life as you grew older? No matter how busy you were, you'd find time to do whatever it took to recover. In truth, that's the prognosis for all underearners—you have a degenerating condition that will hinder your quality of life as you age.

> "Money is a guarantee that we can have what we want in the future."
>
> —*Aristotle*

Once you decide to make overcoming underearning a priority, your whole perspective is likely to change. When you know exactly what you want, it becomes easier to figure out what you need to do. The way becomes clear. A problem that once seemed overwhelming will become just another thing that needs to be handled. "It felt so daunting before the class," one woman told me about her credit card debt, "but somehow paying it down wasn't that hard. I just did what I had to do."

And from this one decision springs a whole series of smaller choices. Do you pay down your debt, or buy a new dress? Do you raise your rates, or find reasons not to risk? Do you look for a better job, or put up with the low pay? Do you listen to naysayers, or stick to your guns? When you have a profit motive, every decision, no matter how tough, becomes as clear as whether or not to put on your oxygen mask first.

Similarly, Kathy Forbes, a dental hygienist turned consultant told me, "I decided not to get caught up in stuff that doesn't produce income. I feel guilty that I can't give more time to volunteer work. But I have to look out for me. It's hard, but sometimes you have to make hard decisions."

STICKIN' TO YOUR GUNS. . . .

Kathleen White, a casualty of a corporate layoff, had one goal in mind: to find a better job that paid more money and was close to home. "I decided on a very high amount and got very focused. Even though people were telling me 'Get off your high horse, you're going to have to take a pay cut. Things are bad—we're in a recession,' I just kept saying no, I am worth it, and if there's a terrific job out there, I might as well be the one to get it."

When offered a job for less money, she briefly considered it as a temporary stopgap. "But two hours later I got a phone call from a recruiter about a job eight minutes from my house. Although I didn't hit my high-end salary goal, I negotiated for more money than I was making before. I'm on the senior management team, working with wonderful people. I have a whole new lease on life. It's exactly what I wanted. I can't tell you how happy I am. And it's so close that sometimes I go home for lunch!"

She's adamant when she says: "The whole key for me was the decision I made at the beginning [make more money and work closer to home]. When I felt the doubts coming, I decided that's not where I'm going. I just kept thinking, 'The best thing is going to happen for me.' If a job I was interested in didn't work out, I'd say, 'Okay, I'm going to give myself a day to feel really bad and that's it.' I focused on my goal. I wrote affirmations. I listened to tapes." She held to her decision, whatever it took, despite "the fear nipping at my heels."

Exercise:
Making Your Decision

In the space below, write this sentence: IT'S TIME TO MAKE MORE MONEY. The sheer act of writing starts programming your unconscious.

Now, read what you wrote, out loud, three times—each time with more conviction!

Next, complete the following sentence, then write the sentence in the space below.

THIS YEAR I WILL MAKE $ _____.

Write out the sentence stating how much you'll make:

How did you feel writing these sentences?

Was it difficult? Easy?

Did it feel uncomfortable? Perfectly natural?

Did you notice any resistance?

Look back to the sentences you completed on pages 82 and 84. Do you find any information that would shed light on why you might have previously decided not to make more money?

For "bonus points," tell someone else, if you haven't already, exactly what dollar amount you wrote down. How does it feel to talk about it? (If you're too shy to say aloud what you want to make, you'll have another chance when we get to the next step.)

WHICH IS IT—THE COMFORT MOTIVE
OR THE PROFIT MOTIVE?

I can just hear your protests as I write. "It can't be that simple. Just say what you want and poof—the money will flow?"

How many times have you said those very words you just wrote—*"It's time to make more money"*—and nothing happened? In fact, the world is filled with people who swear they want more, tell it to anyone who'll listen, beseech the gods, even beg on the streets. Surely they made the decision. So why are they left hanging?

The reason is simple, but not always clear because it has to do with an internal contradiction. I call it the **Grand Conundrum,** a deeply embedded, rarely conscious, internal conflict, often between the comfort motive and profit motive.

The Grand Conundrum

You get what you *really* want, *not* what you ask for.

Dave Elvin, a voice-over artist, described it this way: "There's this place I really want to get to, a lifestyle, an income. And at the same time, I'm comfortable where I am. I just want to stare at my computer and take jobs that trickle in."

Like Dave, you may say you want more, but if you'd rather be safe and stay comfortable, are scared of what prosperity may do to your life, distrust the people who are wealthy, don't believe you deserve it, or see money as the root of all evil, then abundance isn't really what you want. This sets up an inner discord that's inscrutable, insidious, and often crazy-making. It also explains why affirmations, as powerful as they are, don't always work.

This Grand Conundrum is a normal human condition. According to psychologist Abraham Maslow, we all have two forces inside us. One clings to safety. The other pushes us forward. As long as the former remains subliminally stronger, you're likely to find yourself hopelessly stuck.

How do you know what you truly want? Look at what is happening in your life now. If this is not what you say you want, then chances are good your goals are in conflict. For example, if you've been saying for years you want more money, but your bank balance hasn't gone past double digits, then deep down, you don't actually want what you're asking for. Somewhere along the way, you made a subconscious decision that opposes your declared intention.

The solution? Realize you made the wrong decision. Then make a different decision, consciously. You might start by deciding to make money, but you may find there's a more fundamental decision that has to come first.

Cheri Schell, who had a big surge in income, spoke for many: "I thought the decision was to make more money. No, that wasn't it. My decision first had to be 'I'm important. I matter. I put myself first.'"

> "A decision is a conclusion based on everything you believe about yourself."
> —*A Course in Miracles*

Donna Weaver, a real estate broker from a "teeny tiny" town outside Olympia, Washington, had her single biggest month ever right after the workshop, netting $17,000—up from $5,000 the month before—even though she had set her goal for less. "We are talking about a huge difference in my income," she exclaimed. "I had to make a decision, 'Am I going to try to help someone who really wants a house, but doesn't have a down payment? Or am I going to focus on people who can afford it?' I had to purposefully decide to quit worrying about taking care of people. I want to be able to help others, but I don't want to be eating macaroni and cheese while giving everything away."

For Cheri, Donna, and countless others, previous decisions—like "put others first," "money is bad," "I'm unworthy"—have to be replaced before the "more money" decision can play out. Discovering those deeper decisions that stem from our earliest experiences can serve as a springboard, catapulting us into a new relationship to money.

The following is a journal-writing exercise to ferret out an important decision you made about money way back in childhood, which you've continued to act on as if it was cast in cement.

The memory could be totally benign or deeply traumatic. But in that moment you made a decision. You had no idea you made it, never discussed it, and assumed it was true, then you lived the rest of your life consistent with that decision.

Journal Exercise

MY EARLIEST MEMORY

Relax, take a deep breath, and let your mind wander back to your childhood, to your earliest memory of money. Take your time. Don't force or censor anything. Just observe whatever pops up. When a memory emerges, take a good look. What are you doing? Who else is there? What exactly is going on? How are you feeling? Now freeze that memory into a snapshot. Open your eyes and journal about it, using the following sentences as guidelines:

My earliest memory is (describe it like a photo) . . .

What decisions did I make in that moment? (If you're not sure, just take a guess.)

In my earliest memory, I'm maybe five years old, standing on a step stool in front of the sink, brushing my teeth. I have just asked my mother how much money she has, and she won't tell me. At that moment, I realize now, I made a decision: it's bad to talk about money.

That one decision—it's bad to talk about money—got me into serious financial trouble as an adult, and explains why, in the beginning, I had so much anxiety writing about finances. The second I recognized it, I made a new decision: it's important to talk about money, and the more open I am, the more people I can help.

The second step of overcoming underearning is to make decisions that will better serve your desire to earn more.

YOUR DEEPEST VALUES

Another source of the Grand Conundrum comes when you're not living according to your values. Values are those ideals that you cherish most in life, like family, spiritual growth, or independence. When you attempt to do something that's inconsistent with or doesn't include your values, the goal loses its luster, you lose your motivation. Decisions become so much easier to carry out when there's no dispute between our values and our goals. Problem is, many of us haven't a clue what we value most in life. And then we wonder what's missing. I learned how important it is to identify and prioritize my values when I interviewed six-figure women. The ones who were most satisfied with their lives and had the most balance, while making good money, actually took the time to prioritize their values, and made their decisions accordingly.

> "If you ask me what I've come to do, it is this: to live out loud."
>
> —*Émile Zola*

Here's an exercise on page 98 I believe may be the most important one you will do in this book.

Values Clarification

Below is a list of values. Circle ten that are most important to you. If you don't see an important value on this list, add it. Give yourself time to really explore and think about these.

achievement	freedom	justice	security
acceptance	friendship	kindness	self-esteem
adventure	fun	knowledge	self-discipline
aging well	generosity	leadership	service
beauty	God	learning	simplicity
brotherhood	growth	leaving a legacy	spirituality
charity	happiness	leisure	strength
comfort	harmony	life partner	success
community	health	love	support
commitment	honesty	making a	surrender
communication	honor	difference	time alone
courage	humility	parenting	transformation
creativity	independence	patriotism	travel
democracy	individuality	peace	truth
dignity	influence	physical activity	using my talents
discovery	inner peace	power	wisdom
diversity	integrity	respect	others
education	intimacy	responsibility	
family	joy	retirement	

Cross out five that you circled and rank the five that remain in order of importance.
My Most Important Values

1.

2.

3.

4.

5.

Now that you know what values are most important to you, from this point on, before making any decisions, before saying YES or NO to anything, ask yourself this question: Will this get me closer, or take me farther, from my living my values?

IN THE WAKE OF YOUR DECISION . . .

Once you make a conscious and solid decision, three things will happen: coincidences, changes in other areas of your life, and resistance. Guaranteed.

1. Coincidences.

I once heard someone say, "You need to be stubborn about the results you're going for, but very flexible on how you get there." It's so true. Decisions are like magnets. They draw opportunities to you, often disguised as a synchronistic, or coincidental, event. You turn on the news, step on the bus, bump into a friend, hear the phone ring, and from absolutely nowhere, someone or something shows up that's just what you need.

That's exactly what happened to voice-over artist Dave Elvin when he resolved to start valuing himself more. "The *next week,* I suddenly had more work than I could handle. I am not into that woo-woo stuff. But I got calls out of the blue that brought in over $2,000."

> "Coincidences are God's way of acting anonymously."
>
> —*Source unknown*

Kathleen Zacarias, age twenty-five, was equally skeptical. "I didn't believe your comments about making a decision, declaring an intention. It just sounded so New Age. But it's true. It really works."

Kathleen had a high-paying job in the high-tech industry, but wasn't happy. She wanted to be doing more to help people, but "I came from an environment where helping people and making money don't go hand in hand."

I'm proud to say it was a quote by Carl Jung in *Secrets of Six-Figure Women,* "If better is to come, good must stand aside," that moved her to quit. "Declaring your intention and telling people around you is really amazing," she said. Before she even left her old job, she found a new one as network manager for United Way of Metropolitan Atlanta. "It's a nonprofit, helps the community, but runs like a business, and I'm actually making more money, have more responsibilities and opportunities to develop as a person and professional."

As I've seen over the years, this is an inexplicable process—if we tell the truth, decide what we want, then get out of our own way, it's mind-boggling what will happen.

E-mail from Workshop Participant

Barbara,

I attended your May 20 Overcoming Underearning™ workshop. My attendance was actually funded by someone else who wanted to empower women financially.

You stated that once you are committed to earning what you are worth and you make it known, "things" happen for you. Well, [your colleague] Marcia (bless her heart) embarrassed me into telling the whole group what I wanted. I thought about what I wanted all night and the next morning I decided to target a search for only jobs that met my criteria. I immediately found the perfect job. The closing date had passed, but I called them up and they had not yet started processing, so I quickly did up an application and drove it in. I prepared well for the interview and today they called and offered me the job!!!

My whole outlook on work has changed. I will never settle for less than I am worth again. I am also committed to helping other women achieve their goals. I'm not too sure yet how I will accomplish this, but I'm sure now that I have said it out loud, a perfect opportunity will come my way soon!

Thanks again

Judy Maddox

Journal Exercise

Keep a running list of coincidences. Even so-called "bad" experiences can, in the long run, have positive outcomes. Now that you're aware, are you seeing more synchronicity occurring than before? Why do you think that is?

2. Changes in other areas of your life.

You can't segment your life, slice it up like a pizza, and expect nothing to be different but your paycheck. As one woman told me, "Taking charge of money really shakes up your life." Sometimes the changes are positive, like losing weight or having more leisure. Other times, they don't seem so rosy. Relationships turn rocky, your job goes sour, life in general feels out of control. But it's by dealing with those breakdowns, whatever they are, that breakthroughs occur. Change is an inevitable by-product of your plan to overcome underearning. Your task is to go with the flow rather than stick to the status quo.

Journal Exercise

Are any other parts of your life being "shaken up"? How does what's happening apply to your underearning? What are the lessons you're learning?

3. Resistance

There's a law of physics that says for every action, there's an equal and opposite reaction. Every time you commit to a goal, something inside you refuses to comply. Resistance emerges as soon as you enter the **Discomfort Zone,** the space between where you are now and where you want to be. Trying to navigate this space may feel like you're paddling a canoe in a tempest. The natural reaction will be to return to dry land. Resistance kicks in so we can stay comfy. Resistance is always strongest at the very beginning and right before you reach your goal. Those are the times you're most vulnerable to backsliding.

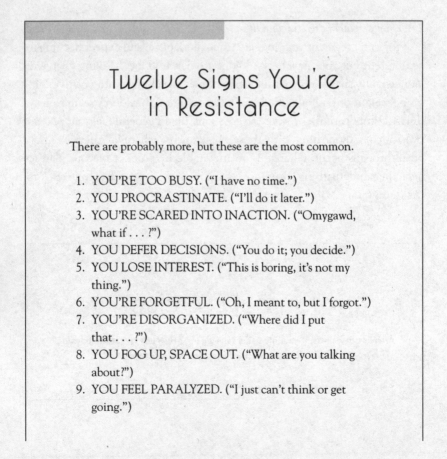

Twelve Signs You're in Resistance

There are probably more, but these are the most common.

1. YOU'RE TOO BUSY. ("I have no time.")
2. YOU PROCRASTINATE. ("I'll do it later.")
3. YOU'RE SCARED INTO INACTION. ("Omygawd, what if . . . ?")
4. YOU DEFER DECISIONS. ("You do it; you decide.")
5. YOU LOSE INTEREST. ("This is boring, it's not my thing.")
6. YOU'RE FORGETFUL. ("Oh, I meant to, but I forgot.")
7. YOU'RE DISORGANIZED. ("Where did I put that . . . ?")
8. YOU FOG UP, SPACE OUT. ("What are you talking about?")
9. YOU FEEL PARALYZED. ("I just can't think or get going.")

10. YOU FIND REASONS NOT TO ACT. ("I can't because . . .")
11. YOU'RE IMPATIENT. ("This is taking way too long.")
12. YOU KEEP RUNNING INTO NAYSAYERS. (Other people say, "You can't do that," "That's not possible." This form of resistance is especially sneaky. You project your own fear out onto others.)

As you proceed with the work of overcoming underearning, see if you find yourself using any of these excuses. Know you're in resistance. You crave the comfort of the familiar. It may be time to make a new decision.

"Part of it is identifying the moment of decision when something happens around money and I see my old pattern," Marvella McPartland told me. "Whenever I got money, I'd make an unhealthy decision, like spend it unwisely, give it away, or lose it, whatever. Now I have become aware of that moment and realize that I can take a deep breath, think more clearly, and decide, 'It's okay to receive this money.' "

One man described his bout with resistance this way: "It felt almost like a tightness in my chest. It was like being in a traffic jam, a mix of 'I don't want to' and 'I can't get out of it.' I just breathed through it and committed to doing something, which I did. I stood back from it and asked, 'Okay, what's the message here? What is this telling me? What's the resistance?' "

Decoding Resistance

★ All resistance comes from fear.
★ At the core of all fear is a belief.
★ At the root of each belief is a decision you made.
★ These decisions are made early, often unconsciously, and have little to do with reality.
★ To ride out the resistance, redo your decision.

The following exercise is a visualization or guided mediation process, to help you identify and uncover what may be getting in the way of reaching your goal. You will be talking to different parts of yourself: your child, your adolescent, your future self, and your negative ego. In my experience, this exercise can be extraordinarily effective in unlocking the mystery to why you're underearning.

Exercise: Talking to Myself

Let yourself relax. Close your eyes. Take a few deep breaths, blowing out any tension, breathing in relaxation. When you're ready, ask yourself the following questions, one at a time. Take a few moments to reflect, then write down the answer to the first one. Do the same with the next two.

How much do I want to make?

Why do I want to make that?

Why don't I want to make that?

Again, close your eyes, let the preceding questions float away, and just relax, taking several deep, slow breaths. Next you're going to imagine that you're talking to different parts of yourself. This exercise takes some time. Don't rush. Do all the stages as suggested here.

First, picture your grown-up self having a conversation with your self as a child, say, five to ten years old. Tell her what you want, and ask her opinion. Listen carefully to what she has to say. Does she have any concerns, advice, comments, or reactions? When you're ready, thank her for coming, watch her leave, then open your eyes and write down what she said in the appropriate space.

Do the same thing with your self as a teenager. Close your eyes, see your self at age thirteen or so. Tell your adolescent self what you want, and hear what she tells you. When she's finished, thank her and say goodbye, open your eyes, and write her response.

Repeat the process with your negative ego, who often looks like a critical parent, or some personification of negativity.

Finally, with closed eyes, picture yourself sometime in the future, perhaps five years from now. Again, tell your future self your goal, and so on.

What does my child self say?

What does my adolescent self say?

What does my negative ego say?

What does my future self say?

Finally, come back to yourself, as you are, after having these dialogues, and answer the following question.

Why *will* I let myself make what I want?

What did you discover? Any surprises?

This exercise can generate tremendous insights. For example, graphic designer Kristen Marie Schuerlein told me, "I had a breakthrough that was so amazingly profound. I saw this little girl around six or seven. I realize it's me. She's skipping, her blonde pigtails flying, with big red bows in her hair, totally cute, as happy as can be. She walks up and whispers, 'You are going to have the most amazing life. You are going to be wealthy, successful, and accomplished.'

"Me at sixteen had short spiky platinum hair, and an attitude that would run all day. I loved that part of my life. She walks up to me and says, 'You are going to have an amazing life. But the wealthier you become, the lonelier you will be.'

"I instantly started to cry. I felt it in my chest, this belief I had been carrying around that the more successful I am, the more isolated I would be. I saw how I'd been stopping myself from taking risks or at least being proactive about my own finances. Who wants to be rich alone?"

What did you do? I asked her.

"I saw the belief was there, acknowledged it, and decided not to operate out of it anymore. I realized it's ridiculous. I'm never going to be alone. I stopped holding myself back. I'm willing to take risks now."

Kristen's words—"I stopped holding myself back. I'm willing to take risks now"—foreshadow the work we'll be doing in the following chapter, Step 3.

CHAPTER FIVE HIGHLIGHTS

- ★ The second step is **making a decision,** or declaring a profit motive.
- ★ You don't need a plan in place. A decision is like a magnet. It'll draw opportunities to you.
- ★ If you're stuck, it may be the Grand Conundrum, the internal battle between what you *say* you want and what you *really* want.
- ★ The solution: make a new decision congruent with your spoken goals and start living according to your values.
- ★ Three things will happen when you make a firm decision: coincidences, changes in other areas of your life, and resistance. Take advantage of the coincidences; don't let other changes throw you; and make sure the resistance doesn't stop you.

Conversation with Myself

What am I afraid will happen if I make more money? What is my fear telling me? What do I believe about myself or the world that activates this fear? What decision led to this belief? Why did I decide that? Where did it come from? What have I gained from holding this belief? What new reality do I want to create? What new decision can I make that will create this reality?

SIX

Step 3:
Stretch

"The question I ask every day is the same it's always been. How much further can I stretch to reach my fullest potential?"

—*Oprah Winfrey*

THE GREAT DIVIDE

As soon as former radio DJ Dave Elvin decided to raise his rates, he got a call to do a voice-over. Normally, he charged $125 a session. This time he wanted to ask for $350. But getting the words out of his mouth was a whole other matter.

"My brain was going no, no, you can't ask for that," he recalled, feeling suddenly daunted by the gaping distance between making a decision and actually doing it.

"It's like you're standing at a precipice, and the place you've got to get to is eight feet away, but your legs only stretch six feet. You've got to get from here to there, so what do you do?"

He did the smart thing and took the third step. He **stretched.** To paraphrase writer Ray Bradbury, relying on faith, he jumped off the cliff and built his wings on the way down. In other words, he did what he thought he couldn't do.

"It was tough saying $350," Dave admitted. "You're not going to be on solid ground for a second, and it's going to be scary."

What happened when he did?

"The guy asked what that price included. I told him what I'd do. He said, 'Cool.' Now I'm wishing I had asked for $500."

Whenever you decide to do something different—whether it's making money or losing weight—the desired result always lies just beyond reach, in the Discomfort Zone. The only way you'll get there is by taking the third step—stretching beyond what feels comfortable to what may seem impossible, doing what you think you can't do.

> "When I saw the title, I thought it was about flying. And I hate flying. But the more something scares me, the more I want to explore it."
>
> —*Director Martin Scorsese about his reaction to the script for* **The Aviator**

While the first two steps in this plan are meant to wake you up, this step demands you get out of bed, whether you feel like it or not. The stretch carries with it this strict stipulation: feel the fear, endure the discomfort, observe the resistance, and *go for it anyway*.

"We are taught that fear is something to avoid at all cost," Sally Beckett told me. "Since the workshop, I've started listening to my gut. If it says, 'You're afraid of this', I say, 'That's a good thing. I'm going toward it. It'll force me to change and grow.' "

HOW DO YOU KNOW
WHEN IT'S TIME TO STRETCH?

The signal to stretch comes in a variety of forms: you're assigned a project that feels out of your league; you're passed over for a promotion that was certainly yours; your new client sets an unreasonable deadline; a seeming coincidence sends you in a new direction; or a gut feeling says that you should talk with your spouse, ask for a raise, or get out and network. No matter how fervently Blanche argues, or how nervous you feel, these opportunities—though they may feel more like ordeals—are the stepping-stones that will take you to the next level.

But before you get there, you'll find yourself smack dab in the Discomfort Zone, an unpredictable passage where—maybe only for a moment, maybe for what seems like forever—your fate feels like a coin toss. You could succeed with a flourish or fall flat on your face. And you're forced to make a choice: Do I stay with what is comfortable? Or do I go where I fear? If you opt for the latter, you'll probably want to zip through it as quickly as possible. But that's not the way it works. The Discomfort Zone has its own pace, and it's different for everyone. But keep in mind: the discomfort is short-lived, but the rewards can be life changing.

We met Laurie, who started a business unpacking for people who are moving, in chapter 4. She did a remarkable job of straightening out her finances because, she said, "I forced myself to talk to a financial counselor and read every financial statement that came in the mail. I am a very results-oriented person. Once I decide to do something, I want it to be finished. I want to say: Yes, I did it, it's done. Unfortunately, you can't do that. You have to go through the process."

There's no escaping the Discomfort Zone. It's unsettling, filled with tension, and believe me, you'll be tested. You'll find yourself wavering, all set to forge ahead but oh so tempted to stay where it's safe. Emotional vacillation is a common reaction when you're teetering on the brink, or in the full throes of a stretch.

Becky Corlis, an attractive, soft-spoken single mom in her fifties, quit her job as a sales assistant in a financial firm to go into real estate, where "I could decide my value, not let someone else do it." When she gave her three-weeks notice, her boss begged her to stay longer since she was going on vacation. Becky refused. Her boss was enraged.

"It was a stare-down, an actual stare-down," Becky recalled. "I just looked right back at her. There was one moment I was sure I was going to cave in. And before, I would have. I would've said, 'Okay, whatever you want. I am here to make your life easier,' thinking that was the more spiritual thing to do. Now I realize I have a voice. I don't have to be this mousy person stuck in a corner. So I said, 'This isn't convenient for me. I have given you enough time, and that's it.' This was her problem, not mine."

Then, after a moment's pause in our interview, I watched the old Becky sneak back in as she added apologetically, "I sound so bad, don't I?"

"Why do you think that?" I asked, not surprised by the predictable relapse.

"It feels so heartless, and embarrassing," she stammered. Then, hearing her words, she snapped back to her senses. "Wait! I'm not responsible for everyone else's happiness. That's a lie. They are grown up. They choose the way they want to be, and I get to choose what's right for me. It's not comfortable, it's scary, but that's okay. Afterwards, I actually felt wonderful."

Six-Month E-mail Update from Becky

"I want you to know that your seminar helped me tremendously. I am doing very well in Real Estate. I am so happy I took this 'scary risk' and made this change in my life. It was the best thing I could have ever done for myself. I love it! Now that I have taken a risk, I realize that the rewards are unsurpassable! Even if I would fail in the future, I will not accept defeat. I will keep getting up as many times as it takes to see myself as a successful person, not only financially, but one who helps others by how I live my life."

YOUR ONLY *REAL* BARRIER

When you get right down to it, there's only one thing that stands between your decision to make more money and actually having it. It's not your job, your children, your spouse, your age, your gender, your lack of credentials, or whatever you thought it was.

Your biggest barrier is fear.

There's nothing wrong with being afraid. Fear is normal. We all have it. *Fear is the natu-*

"Where the heart is willing, it will find a thousand ways; where it is unwilling, it will find a thousand excuses."

—*Arlen Price*

Journal Exercise

Journal your response to this question: If you were *not* acting out of fear, what would you do?

ral reaction to real or perceived danger. But the operative word here is "perceived."

I once got an e-mail that gave me a good laugh while vividly making this point: "I can jump out of an airplane, but take control of my life and make more money, now that's a REAL challenge."

WHAT'S YOUR STRETCH?

From this day forward, find ways to stretch on a regular basis. You are training yourself to surpass former limitations. Every day, actually seek opportunities to:

★ do what you think you can't do (be it as simple as adding a lap to your swimming routine or as difficult as competing in a triathlon);
★ speak up and ask for what you want (whether it's the last cookie on the plate or your coworker to turn down the radio);
★ let go of what's holding you back (anything from an unhealthy relationship to a directive from Blanche).

What can you start doing *right now* that will take you out of your comfort zone? It may have nothing to do with work or money. The idea is to find ways to empower yourself by pushing yourself.

Exercise:
My Personal Stretch

What are some things I could be doing that I've been afraid to do? (Make sure one of them is to tell someone else your earning goal. You've got to be able to confidently declare your intention without laughing, explaining, or getting embarrassed.)

List ideas below.

For example, actress Rae Kraemer, age twenty-nine, had racked up $50 in late fees at the video store. Instead of paying it off, she negotiated with the manager. He reduced it to $20. "I never would've done that before. It was because of what you said: *you don't get what you deserve, you get what you demand.* Usually, I'm horribly embarrassed to do something like that. It actually felt good. I just felt a lot more empowered."

Another woman, middle-aged, went out and bought thong underwear, something she'd always wanted to wear but had been too afraid of how she might look or what her husband would think. Turns out he loved it, and so did she. "It's my little secret that makes me feel powerful," she said with a big grin.

FLEXING YOUR MUSCLES

The stretch is not about eliminating fear. It's about acting in spite of it. Your potential, like tight muscles, needs to be stretched. How else will you build up your confidence?

Katana Abbott, a Michigan financial advisor already making six figures, readily admitted she was undercharging and her business wasn't growing, because "I realized that I was sabotaging myself by not asking what I was worth." But after the workshop, she shored up her courage and bumped up her fees.

"It is not because things are difficult that we do not dare, it is because we do not dare that things are difficult."

—*Seneca*

"It was like magic," she exclaimed. "As soon as I did this, I felt better about myself, and new clients had no trouble with the higher prices. I almost think my fees were too low and discounted what I did in their eyes. Now with my confidence up, my business is growing, and I'm attracting new clients effortlessly. I really believe that when we change the way we think, the world will change around us."

And also within us. Stretching is like helium for our self-esteem. As someone once said, *"Confidence is a memory of success."* Even if a stretch didn't pay off, the most successful remained undeterred. One woman even sang aloud, "I just pick myself up, I dust myself off, and I start all over again." It could be the theme song for all the Doers I interviewed, the ones who achieved remarkable results.

"I've always had a lot of problems with fear," Rae Kramer told me. However, this surprisingly timid young woman had an incredible transformation in a very short time.

"Before the class, I thought courage was something completely different. I thought it meant not being afraid. Since I learned that everybody is afraid, but the courageous people act anyway, my life has dramatically changed. I've been taking more chances, feeling more confident, and have had much more success."

Rae's first stretch was to quit her teaching job. "It was hard," she recalled. "It paid well and I'm so afraid of upsetting people. But I was having to turn down acting jobs."

Since she quit, her work and her income has stayed steady, because, she admits, "I'm beginning to ask for higher pay," but more important, she's stopped "chickening out of auditions."

Rae is living proof that facing your fear is the key to success. For example, right after the workshop, she auditioned for a children's show that she didn't realize was a musical. "I was terrified because I'd have to sing. Part of me really wanted to skip it.* But I kept hearing what you said about feeling the fear and doing it anyway. So I did the audition, sang the best I could. I didn't get the part, but the fact that I was able to face my fear opened up a whole new door for me in the theater realm. It means I can do it again. I expect the next time to be a lot easier."

At about the same time, Rae auditioned for Shakespeare in the Park, even though it conflicted with a show she was currently in but doing for no pay. "Normally, I never would've tried out for it because it might mean I'd have to tell someone I can't do their show. I didn't want to make them feel bad. But this one paid, and I really wanted to do it. I'm so happy I did. I got the part. It turned out to be a much better experience, which opened a lot of doors for me."

> "Ultimately we know deeply that the other side of every fear is freedom."
>
> —*Marilyn Ferguson*

Though, at the time of our interview, Rae hadn't yet met her stated goal of $50,000 a year, I knew she was no longer an underearner. "I have so much less fear since I started this process. I've been pushing myself to stop resisting, to do things that I'm afraid of. I've felt so much better about life in general ever since."

---

* This is too ironic not to share. Rae has been singing in a rock band for years! Still, she was terrified of having to learn songs on the spot without time to practice.

E-mail Update from Rae, Seven Months Later

"Barbara, I really have to thank you. Since our interview I have had even more success. Because of the calculated risks I've learned to take, and courage you have taught me, I have started making a name for myself in this town. I've received great reviews in all of the local papers. I've received offers for four roles in different shows this last month and I only auditioned for one of them. I've also been asked to join another rock band, one that pays $2000 per gig. And, I am about to face my biggest fear, and direct a show. I never would have asked to do that before learning how to be truly courageous. Thanks to you I am well on my way to meeting my monetary goals."

Bottom line, *overcoming underearning isn't measured solely by the amount of money you make, but the degree to which your life is no longer run by fear.*

Becky Corlis told me that her son's car broke down recently, and he wanted to borrow hers. "Normally, I'd say, 'That's fine, I'll cancel my plans.' But I didn't do that. I told him, 'I need my car. You'll have to find another ride.' " Her son was shocked. So was Becky. "It just shot out of my mouth. But I didn't want to be a doormat anymore. I didn't want him to see me as one. And I certainly don't want him treating other women as doormats either. I've been such a people pleaser that it got ridiculous."

FIND YOUR AUTHENTIC VOICE—AND USE IT TO SPEAK UP

Whenever you speak your truth, you're bound to rattle some cages. Many people would rather stay underearners than risk ruffling someone's feathers. This is understandable. Speaking up can be scary. It was for me. I had to raise my prices, bargain harder, and turn down jobs that didn't pay. This sort of thing is difficult for most people, but especially for women.

Studies prove that men who are forceful and assertive win higher marks and more respect from their boss. Women who are forceful and assertive are downgraded and referred to as bitches. But if I've learned one thing from successful women, it is this: *being a bitch is NOT a bad thing.*

I'm not referring to the codependent self that forfeits her needs and gets very cranky, or the fearful self that can turn mean and start bullying. I'm talking about the Authentic Self who knows who she is, has the courage to take a stand, and refuses to be a victim or put up with abuse. *That* bitch.

Any time you ask for what you want, say no to what you don't, and step into the unknown with your head high and shoulders straight, you claim your power, you embrace your bitch. That's when you become a "Babe in Total Control of Herself," as I had emblazoned on a T-shirt not long ago.

In fact, while writing this chapter, I got a call from a corporate lawyer who'd just informed a client she was raising her fees modestly. He was taken aback, but agreed. She felt terrible. "I feel bad," she told me. "My fees are fair. I had been undercharging him. But he's upset. Now I don't feel right."

My response: "It's okay to feel bad. It's okay to feel guilty. It's okay to have regrets. *Just don't let those feelings stop you.* This has nothing to do with money. It's about valuing yourself. And if you're not used to asking what you're worth, it's going to feel uncomfortable in the beginning. Take this 'feel bad' as a sign you're going in the right direction."

This may sound obvious, but the most efficient way for entrepreneurs to overcome underearning is to raise their prices. Surprisingly, this comes as a revelation to many, and a source of resistance to most. They're terrified they'll lose clients. But in my experience, and as you'll read in this book, when you value yourself, people automatically put a higher value on you, too.

> "It's time to stop destroying the inner bitch in ourselves. Stop apologizing for her. Set her free."
> —Elizabeth Hilts

The same holds true if you're working for someone else. You have to negotiate for more, whether you're taking a new job or requesting a raise. Think about this. Linda Babcock, in *Women Don't Ask: Negotiation and the Gender Divide*, writes that "a woman who routinely negotiates her salary increases will earn over one million dollars more by the time she retires than a woman who accepts what she's offered every time without asking for more."

Negotiation Tips

A salary offer is not a foregone conclusion. Ninety percent of human resource professionals polled expect salaries to be negotiated. Overcoming
underearning requires that you take a stand, ask for what you want, negotiate until you reach a mutually satisfactory agreement, or walk away where
appropriate. Here are some tips for a successful negotiation.

★ Know what you want. Research the going rates in your field. Ask the
   high end of the spectrum. You can always negotiate down, but never up.
★ "No" means "not now."
★ Negotiate salary only after a job offer. Don't be the first to bring it up.
   "Make them fall in love with you before talking money" (*Wall Street
   Journal*, October 29, 2004).
★ Negotiate more than money: early salary review, signing bonus, reloca-
   tion costs, profit sharing, flexible schedule, paid time off, benefits,
   perks, educational programs, expense account, club memberships,
   bigger office, laptop, cell phone, job title.
★ Act confident (even if you don't feel it). Communicate with authority.
   Perceived confidence has a big impact.
★ Request twenty-four to seventy-two hours to think over the offer.
★ Always start negotiations on a positive note. For example, thank the
   employer for the opportunity and make a counteroffer.
★ If someone acts put off by a reasonable counteroffer, consider it a red
   flag. Perhaps the employer doesn't value what you bring to the table.
★ The best time to negotiate, or renegotiate, is when you have other offers.
★ Get the offer in writing.
★ Above all, focus on relationship building. "It's always harder for someone
   to say 'no' if they know you and like you" (www.WallStreetJournal.com).
★ Practice negotiating with a friend or in the mirror.
★ Have points prepared and build a case around your value and what you
   bring to the company.

LETTING GO

I believe one of the major reasons people get stuck is because they're clinging to the very thing that's holding them in place. Nothing propels us into our Discomfort Zone quicker than letting go. And it's usually that which we're most afraid to let go of that is the very thing we need to release.

> "We must be willing to relinquish the life we've planned, so as to have the life that is waiting for us."
> —Joseph Campbell

As Sally Beckett told me, "My biggest fear was losing my husband, so that's the fear I had to face. I had to be willing to walk away from him if he wasn't on the same path. So I gave him the ultimatum that we choose to be financially responsible and financially successful as a couple or we can't be a couple because the change was going to happen. I was no longer going to tolerate less pay for more work (his or mine), or this huge credit card debt, and if I was taking responsibility for making the changes with money, I had to make it across the board. Fortunately, he had the good sense to come with me."

The moral of Sally's story: you may not need to actually give anything up, but the willingness to do so frees you to take the necessary steps to reach the next level. It boils down to this: Do I let go of what's not serving me or do I abandon myself?

Linda Brown, an events planner, had lost interest in her business. She knew she needed to let it go, but when someone suggested she look for a job, it was a tough call for her to make. She'd been self-employed all her life. Giving up that freedom was scary. Still, she went on interviews, and within weeks a real estate firm made her an offer. Trouble was, it paid less than she wanted.

"I told them I would sleep on it," she said. "They said no, we need to know by the end of the day. I called her later and said, 'I know you want the answer today, but I'm not prepared to give it to you. I still need to sleep on this.' " (The ability to say no is part of the stretch.)

She woke up the next day still dissatisfied with the salary and concerned about working for someone else. She decided to make them "a ridiculous offer. I told them I'd take the job for $20,000 more if they let me be an independent contractor. They said okay. Overnight I became a six-figure woman. Before that I'd never earned more than $50,000. It was about self-respect and self-value. I came into my own by doing this."

In every single interview with a successful person, letting something go—from the trivial to the treasured, from the concrete to the intangible— always factored in.

- ★ A writer let go of playing backgammon on the computer, using the extra time to write more articles.
- ★ An executive let go of drinking a bottle of wine every evening, which enabled her to pursue an MBA.
- ★ A massage therapist let go of her mother's messages that there's never enough and found it changed her relationship with food and money.
- ★ Quite a few let go of anger at themselves, a parent, or former spouse, which freed up energy to devote to their dreams.
- ★ Some let go of a spouse.
- ★ A gallery owner began "cleaning out my house for the first time since the divorce. I gave away a bunch of furniture. I feel like I'm back on track."
- ★ A real estate agent let go of taking business calls at night so she could spend uninterrupted time with her kids.
- ★ A saleswoman "stopped the madness" by letting go of a highly stressful, but lucrative, job to find another that "fit with my values" and paid exactly the same.
- ★ A struggling entrepreneur let go of her dream of becoming a coach to land a fulfilling job with steady pay.
- ★ A number of moms let go of enabling grown children by "being generous to a fault." Then they had to let go of the subsequent guilt when they set stricter boundaries.
- ★ A computer programmer let go of the belief "Someone else will do this for me"; another let go of the "adrenaline rush" that came from living on the edge. Both started taking money management more seriously.

★ Just about everyone let go of devaluing themselves, and instead
   of putting everyone else first, started taking time for themselves.

Exercise: What's on Your Letting-Go List?

In the space below, write down anything you think is holding you back. Brainstorm with yourself. If you're not sure, guess. It can be something tangible like a job, a relationship, or a situation that isn't serving you. Or it can be psychological, like a limiting belief, a destructive emotion, or low self-esteem.

My Letting-Go List

You don't need to do anything with this list yet. Just keep adding to it when something comes to mind.

YOU'LL LIKE THESE STRETCH MARKS

At this point in my workshop, I usually play a song I call the "High Earner's Anthem." It's a tune by Kris Kristofferson, and to me, the chorus sums up the very attitude that separates the Doers from those who remain underearners.

"I'd rather be sorry for something I did, than for something I didn't do."

Stretching takes guts, no doubt about it. That's why the next chapter, the fourth step, is so important. The Brainstorming Exercise on page 124 will give you a sense of just how potent this fourth step can be.

CHAPTER SIX HIGHLIGHTS

★ The third step, **the stretch,** requires you to take action, to enter the Discomfort Zone, to face your fears.

★ To overcome underearning, you actually must seek out opportunities to stretch, to do what you think you can't do.

★ You enter the Discomfort Zone every time you
  1. Do something unfamiliar.
  2. Speak up and ask for what you want.
  3. Let go of what's holding you back.

★ The payoff is not only higher earnings, but, more important, higher self-esteem.

Conversation with Myself

What signals have you been getting that you're ready to stretch? What's stopping you?

Exercise: Brainstorming the Stretch

This exercise is a workshop favorite. Done in small groups, it's a wonderful opportunity for you to get other opinions, generate new ideas, soak up invaluable support, and practice your approach.

Start by thinking of a stretch you want to take, something you've been wanting to do, to say, or to let go of, but have been reluctant or scared to attempt. It need not be career related. It could be:

* ★ asking someone for a date
* ★ ending a relationship with a negative neighbor
* ★ requesting a job lead
* ★ refusing to pay your son's car insurance
* ★ quitting a volunteer position
* ★ taking a trip by yourself

Write your stretch here:

If you aren't already working in a group, find two or three friends you would feel comfortable sharing your stretch with, and who would also be willing to share theirs. You can do this over the phone, but I highly recommend sitting face to face.

First, one of you describes your desired stretch. The others will listen intently, ask questions, then offer comments, advice, feedback, suggestions, resources, even a chance to rehearse.

In the workshop, each person usually gets around seven minutes to be in the "hot seat," but if you have no time restraint, take as long as you want. This exercise is extraordinarily powerful. Be sure to write down helpful feedback or any ideas that come out of it (even when others are in the hot seat).

Ideas I'm taking away:

SEVEN

Step 4: Create Community

"Alone we can do so little; together we can do so much."

—*Helen Keller*

THE MISSING PIECE

At first, I was puzzled. I understood why the Dawdlers, who were at best halfhearted in their efforts to change, remained underearners. But I saw a subcategory emerge among workshop graduates that I couldn't explain. I call them the **Doers Who Didn't.** They were gung ho about getting ahead, made huge strides in all sorts of ways . . . *except* in their earnings.

One woman, whom I'll call Norma, was brimming with enthusiasm when our interview began. "So much has happened. I've gotten a handle on my finances, including making out a will, which I'd been putting off forever. I've started writing my book. I created a new business model. My husband and I have gotten so organized, it's like we're living in a different house." Then she stopped, and I could almost feel her energy drop and frustration creep in. "But I still struggle with the amount I want to be paid. I still feel like an underearner."

Are there some people who are just die-hard underearners, I wondered? Or was there something I wasn't seeing, something that future high earners just naturally had or did that others didn't? When I reread the transcript of our interview, I found the missing piece. Norma, and others like her, had ignored the fourth step.

"Tell me about the people you hang out with," I had asked her later in the interview. "Have you talked to them about what you're doing?"

"Most of my friends are not into money," she said. "Their focus is on getting out in nature, not on earning more. I would never talk to them about this stuff."

"What would happen if you started making more money?" I inquired.

"They'd freak out," she said, laughing.

When I wrote *Secrets of Six-Figure Women*, I saw how critical support was to those women's success. But I honed in on singular sources of support like an inspiring mentor, a respected role model, or a remarkable teacher. What I overlooked was how the sum of all their relationships impacted their potential success. Only during my interviews for this book did I begin to fully grasp the broader scope of this fourth step. Whatever we achieve (or don't) is significantly affected by our cumulative interactions with everyone we associate with on a regular basis. *Just as it takes a village to raise a child, I'm convinced it takes a supportive community to reach the next level.*

Indeed, all of those I've talked to who became high earner's were surrounded by people who cheered them on, held them accountable, modeled what's possible, provided resources, and inspired them to aim higher.

Underearners, on the other hand, either operate in isolation or gravitate to people like themselves. They seem to attract naysayers, pessimists, worrywarts, negative folks who want to hold them back. Not because they're bad people. But they're scared, afraid of change themselves. Trying to increase your income while surrounded by naysayers is like leaving the house with a couple of kids hanging on each leg, begging you not to go. Chances are you won't get very far. Even if you eventually do, it's much harder and takes a whole lot longer.

As one woman admitted during the workshop, "It's really hard not to listen to the voices of people trying to hold you back, unless you have other voices saying something different."

I have come to see that the fourth step, creating a supportive community, is mandatory for two reasons. First of all, change is difficult and requires courage. If the people around you are going to freak out or frown upon your efforts, if there's a chance they'll ridicule or reject you, it's way too easy to throw in the towel. Why invite arguments or risk abandonment when you've got so much support for just staying put?

The other reason is best explained by the old adage "You become who you're with." Not only are we attracted to people like us, we also reshape ourselves, unconsciously mimicking others to feel like we fit in.

> A University of Chicago study reports that "we turn to others not so much for guidance, but for rational construction or confirmation of our own way of seeing things."

WHO'S IN YOUR COMMUNITY?

I've discovered that while support can come from many sources, there are four kinds that are absolutely essential: **True Believers, Confidantes, Way Showers,** and **Messengers.** The fourth step is all about making sure you have plenty of each of them in your life.

The Four Kinds of Supporters

TRUE BELIEVERS comprise your fan club. They recognize your potential, offer encouragement, and celebrate even your tiniest success. Your closest associates should all fit into this category, plus anyone else who's out there rooting for you. They're the ones who say, "Go for it."

continued

CONFIDANTES are your sounding boards. You can talk to them intimately about your attitudes toward money and your efforts to change. They may or may not be on the same path, but they genuinely relate to the steps that you're taking. They're the ones who say, "I understand."

WAY SHOWERS are role models. They provide you with a map or serve as proof that success is possible. They could be current acquaintances, people you've only read about, or someone you've admired from afar. They're the ones who say, or imply, "You can do it, *too*; let me show you how."

MESSENGERS deliver valuable information. They may have a referral, an idea, a job lead, or some communication that provides forward momentum. You may already know them, but mostly you'll meet them through networking. They're the ones who say, "I can help."

Exercise: Who's in Your Community?

Complete the five columns with people in your life who would fit in each category. Take time to really think this through.

TRUE BELIEVERS	CONFIDANTES	WAY SHOWERS	MESSENGERS	NAYSAYERS

How did you feel doing this exercise?

Which list is the longest? Shortest? What does that tell you?

Are there any names you would like to add?

How do the naysayers affect you? What would you like to do about them?

Where could you go to meet new people?

Keep this list handy, refer to it often, keep adding new names, and have frequent contact with those in the first four columns. Consider avoiding those in the fifth.

SIX PRINCIPLES FOR BUILDING
YOUR POWERFUL COMMUNITY

Communities are fluid entities. You can shape them as you choose. Your task is to find people who not only support you as you are now, but also welcome the person you're striving to become—someone personally empowered and financially independent. If in the preceding exercise your first four columns were sparsely populated, or the fifth distressingly full, you may wonder where you'll find your Believers, Confidantes, Way Showers, and Messengers.

> "Our chief want in life is somebody who shall make us do what we can."
>
> —*Ralph Waldo Emerson*

I've got the answer for you. Here are six principles that I promise will enable you to create a powerful community of supportive people.

Principle #1—Realize no one will do this for me, but I don't have to do it alone.

This is the Inner Work of the fourth step. To create a powerful community, you first need the appropriate mind-set.

I am convinced the number one reason people fail to achieve financial success is because deep down they secretly hope someone or something will swoop down and save them. The Prince Charming syndrome is insidious in our society.

"I kept expecting my husband to manage my finances," Kathy Forbes exclaimed. "But I decided I couldn't wait for him to find the time or desire. So I had to take the bull by the horns. I had to take control of the finances."

> "A Man Is Not a Financial Plan."
>
> —*Bumper sticker, from www.wife.org*

Women aren't the only ones waiting for a white knight. Nor is Prince Charming necessarily a man. Prince Charming is whatever we believe will bail us out or take care of us in the future: the lottery, an inheritance, a hot tip, or just an amorphous something we've never labeled but subconsciously rely on.

This kind of thinking neither attracts powerful people, nor does it empower you personally. Trying to overcome underearning while harboring a rescue fantasy is like training for a marathon by watching a video, then jogging once around the block. You won't have the stamina to go the distance.

But dispelling the rescue myth is only half the equation. Without the second part of this realization, "I don't have to do it alone," you

> **"Isolation is a dream killer."**
> —*Barbara Sher*

can easily fall victim to the Lone Ranger complex. Underearners often operate in a vacuum, convinced they have to do everything by themselves. Delegating, networking, or soliciting help are foreign concepts in their daily lives. But as six-figure earner Karen Page told me, "Success is a social activity. You can't do it alone, you just can't."

E-mail Update from Realtor Donna Weaver

"Last month I hired a bookkeeper to take care of my monthly finances since I spend so much time worrying about that part. Now, I can think about what I do best (real estate and investments) while someone else takes control of the checkbook. WHEW. I can honestly say that finding I am not the only female who freezes when the words "balance your checkbook" are uttered was a turning point. Being brave enough to quit giving away my money is now at the top of my list, while balancing the checkbook is at the top of my bookkeeper's. Which is the way it should be."

"I was taught you have to do everything yourself," Jason Beckett told me. "Don't ask for help. Keep everything to yourself. But that's a trap. If I had found someone in my previous business who could've taken care of the core while I was off doing other things, then that business would still be thriving."

Principle #2   Reach out, ask for support.

Jason kept his day job in retail while setting up his new business designing furniture. When a store customer mentioned his background was marketing, Jason asked to meet him for coffee. "I just wanted to find out what he knew, who he knew, what was available. He got excited and wanted to be part of the team. That just reinforced the lesson I've learned over the past couple of years. The info, the people, the knowledge are all available. You are responsible for going out and finding it. At first it felt awkward. I would prefer to just quietly go about my business. But that doesn't get results. You have to understand that there are people who have done what you're trying to do and may have a different face on it.

> "Remember, we all stumble, every one of us. That's why it's a comfort to go hand in hand."
>
> —*Emily Kimbrough*

"My business has played out differently than I expected, because of being willing to talk to other people. Someone connected me with a major furniture distributor. Now we're developing a relationship where, hopefully, they're going to be our distributor and do our marketing."

Sometimes helping hands pop up unexpectedly, at just the right time, like they did for Jason. Other times, we have to go out and find them. More often, as in the following example, we'll be doing both.

The second time Dee Piziak was passed over for promotion, she was crushed. "A very good friend inside the company called and said, 'I heard the news. You need to keep your chin up and reexamine the whole situation. Here's what I'd like you to do.' " He gave her a list of books on success. Then, every Friday, she and this Way Shower discussed what she had read.

"I embarked on a journey of incredible self-awareness. I really began to examine my values," the Milwaukee resident recalled. "Then I woke up one day from doing all this reading and said, 'This company doesn't value me. I'm playing a game I'm never going to win.' " After twenty-one years in high-tech sales, making very good money, Dee made a dramatic change through sheer courage. "I decided to apply for a job at a top-notch insurance company here in town, knowing it was very difficult to get into, and I'd never worked inside a company, I'd always been in the field."

She called her children's piano teacher, whose father was an officer in the company, and asked for his telephone number.

"I was very scared. I'd never asked anyone for a personal favor before. But I called him, a perfect stranger, and said, 'Mr. Irving, I really want to work for your company.' You know what he said? 'Sure, what do you want to do?' In three weeks, I had a job making the same money, working fewer hours, with much less stress."

Reaching out for help ranks high among the scariest stretches. Even the most intrepid have to force themselves to pick up the phone or go to a meeting.

Remember Kathleen White, who found a higher-paying job after being laid off, despite everyone telling her she'd have to settle for less?

"I got very clear on my intentions. I knew I had to do networking and informational interviews. I hate that stuff. It's really hard for me to ask for help. So I kept saying, 'Feel the fear and go for it anyway. Feel the fear and go for it anyway.' I started calling people who all helped by giving me referrals or a reference. Some of these were powerful people I may not have had contact with for years, but I just went ahead and felt the fear, and called them."

There are all kinds of ways to reach out for help: join organizations, attend seminars, even read autobiographies and inspirational books. Cheri Schell met regularly with "friends who were extremely successful" after she told them about my Overcoming Underearning™ workshop and enrolled their support. Quite a few worked with a coach to keep them on track. Others hired people to clean their house, paint their office, keep their books—things they would've normally done themselves, but delegated to someone else after they realized it wasn't the best use of their time.

My favorite example is Nancy Allin, an energetic fifty-year-old who owns a joint-venture furniture business. Her income, she told me, "has done nothing but climb since the workshop. We're on track to go over a million in sales."

I was impressed. "How did you do it?" I asked.

"Part of it was seeing I had a ceiling. But another big assist was when we hired a salesperson and then a support person. We had been working our butts off, six days a week. I thought to make more I'd have to work harder. To me, there were only two choices: grind myself into the ground to make a buck or have less money and more of a life. The workshop got me to look at that assumption, and others, that were holding me back. Now, my life is more in balance. I'm working less and business is growing. I was at a meeting the other day and a speaker said, 'I have the belief that if somebody else can do what I'm doing, I shouldn't be doing it.' I went 'Woo-hoo.' That is exactly it."

Nancy's E-mail Update, a Year and a Half Later

"We had our biggest year ever last year, and this year is on track to go beyond that. My husband and I are looking at where we can diversify our interests and begin investing in some other venues for multiple streams of income. More of that working less for more stuff—YEAH!"

Principle #3—Hang out with the kind of people you want to be, not who you've been.

As one woman remarked about her more successful acquaintances, "I know when I'm around them, I feel like I can do more." Certainly, achievers are inspiring. But, in some convoluted way, so are the slackers, when they're the dominant force in your own little world.

"There are people who will joyfully greet the person you are becoming."
—*Source unknown*

Every single person who conquered their underearning made a concerted effort to associate with like-minded people—which meant letting go of those who weren't on the same wavelength. As Sally Beckett told me, after she quit various odd jobs to become a full-time writer, "I started listening to the people around me. I heard phrases like 'I can't afford that,' 'We've always just gotten by,' 'If I quit my job I'd starve to death.' I saw this negative thinking all around me. I also saw people who didn't think that way, people who'd say, 'Sure, this is possible,' 'I can make this work.' I saw that the biggest roadblock I faced were people who want to keep you where you are. We had to let go of some friends, replace them with people who had a different attitude."

Elaine Hayes was working in a faith-based organization when she decided to leave the nonprofit world. On her fiftieth birthday, she invited all her friends to a party, where she made an announcement.

"I told them this is a new Elaine. Someday I'd like to give my time away, but right now I have to get myself set financially so I know I'm giving my time and it's *not* being taken."

She then held up my book, *Secrets of Six-Figure Women,* and said, "You've got to read this. It'll explain what has happened to me and where I am now. I realize I have all the characteristics of an underearner. If my life is going to change, I have to face my issues and move forward."

What was their reaction, I wondered.

"They started to fall off like flies," she told me. "People took it personally. Others understood, but it was obvious our relationship had changed. These were great people. They all worked at nonprofits, doing the best they could, justifying, while secretly wondering, why they're not being paid what they're worth. I love them, but I knew I needed to find others operating at the same level I wanted to be at. That was absolutely necessary if I was going to move forward." Last I talked to Elaine, she'd become active in the Institute of Management Consultants, attended events for women in business, and was meeting lots of new people. Moreover, her management consulting practice was, in her words, "on her way to earning six figures."

Rest assured, creating a new community doesn't mean banishing people you love from your life. But—and this is a big *but*—you can no longer abandon your self to make everyone else happy. If you're even slightly codependent neglecting your own needs to concentrate on, control, or care take others—you're probably reading this in total horror. But as journalist Harold Swope warns, "I can't tell you the formula for success, but I can give you the formula for failure: try to please everybody."

"The biggest thing I took away from the class was acknowledging the naysayers," Jolee, a forty-five-year-old financial advisor from the Midwest, told me. "My own mother was on the list. Whenever I'm moving ahead, they want to drag me back. I realized maybe it was because I was making them feel uncomfortable, doing something they may want to do or wish they could have."

Her solution? She stopped listening.

"I started using that phrase, 'Thank you for sharing,' and I'd think to myself, 'I don't agree. But I love you anyway.' I'd been trying to convince them why they need to change. That's silly. I've had to let go of needing everyone to be in Jolee's pep club, which is something new for me. I might lose some along the way. But the workshop gave me permission to not be angry and do what I want whether they like it or not."

Principle #4—Recognize the role of the naysayer.

There's a form of support you may not recognize: the naysayer. These pessimists have a purpose. They come into your life for a reason. The Patron Saint of Risk, a benevolent being who wants nothing more than to see you succeed, has personally sent them to you. Every time you decide to do something new, she sends down her Angels of Gloom to shower you with disapproval. The more tentative you feel, the gloomier they sound. If they succeed in dissuading you, be glad. Your commitment, your passion, your desire simply weren't strong enough to do what it takes to get what you want. (In which case, you might want to revisit the previous three steps.)

> "You have no friends. You have no enemies. You have only teachers."
>
> —*Chinese saying*

If you're still determined, regardless of their bad tidings, then you win the Saint's blessing. You've got what it takes to break new ground. And if you're really sharp, you found some food for thought in the crumbs of their criticism.

Darlene was already a successful financial executive when she checked out my workshop because her company was thinking of sponsoring it (which they did). She wasn't an underearner, being satisfied with her income, and only stayed a few hours.

"I felt I made enough, why should I want more? I was embarrassed to be even thinking about it," she told me. "But a week later, I thought 'why not.' I put a Post-it note on my computer with a really big number I thought was impossible to achieve. People asked about it. I told them what it was. They thought it was cool. But one man, who was important to my job, came up and said in a very patronizing tone, 'What makes you think you can do that?' "

Rather than become discouraged, Darlene grew more determined, and sure enough, she exclaimed, "By the end of the year I came within a few dollars of that amount. It just happened!"

Compare Darlene to Jaime, whose dream was to be a home chef. "Right

after the workshop," Jaime told me, "an amazing synchronicity of events oc-
cured. I met a woman with health problems who needed help with food
preparation. It turned out she's a marketing consultant, and she started helping me turn my idea into a business. She kept encouraging me not to under-
sell myself." Every time Jaime told someone her idea, they were equally
enthusiastic, until she ran into an Angel of Gloom.

"I talked to a nutritionist who didn't get the idea that people sometimes
need extra help in the home," Jaime sighed. "I let her knock down my spirit.
I lost momentum. I put the idea on the back burner."

"You listened to one person who shot your idea down, when everyone
else was excited?" I exclaimed.

She nodded. "I keep telling myself I'll get back to it, but I've been in a
survival mode. I'm just caught up in making it day to day."

No matter how bold you may be, it's easy to lose your footing when
you're caught off guard by a naysayer during a weak moment. Should that
happen, the fifth principle will get you back on your feet.

Principle #5—Watch what you talk about.

Language is powerful. There is a direct correlation between the words
that you use and the life that you have.

I saw this principle in action right after I wrote my last book, when the
economy went sour. I noticed I was having very different conversations with
the six-figure women I had kept in touch with than I was having with most
others. Underearners were constantly com-
plaining about the lousy economy, quickly dis-
missing the mere idea of making more money.
But the high earners, even those who had
been hit by hard times, were surprisingly up-
beat about the opportunities that were out
there.

Their words became self-fulfilling prophe-
cies. Their outcomes directly reflected their
differing perspectives.

The secret to standing tall when the sky is
falling, and attracting people who will help

> "Apologizing for uninten-
> tional, low-profile, non-
> egregious errors erodes
> our self-confidence and,
> in turn, the confidence oth-
> ers have in us."
>
> —*Lois Frankel,* author of
> Nice Girls Don't Get
> the Corner Office

prop you up, is this: Watch what you say. *Talk about what you're committed to, not what you're worried about.* Stop apologizing unnecessarily or belittling yourself in any way. Tell people what you want to create and have them hold you accountable. One woman instructed all her friends, "When you hear me making excuses, call me on it."

This is not about positive thinking. It's about the power that words have over your attitude and behavior. Life follows what you say. What you share, you strengthen. What you focus on expands. It's never the other way around. Never!

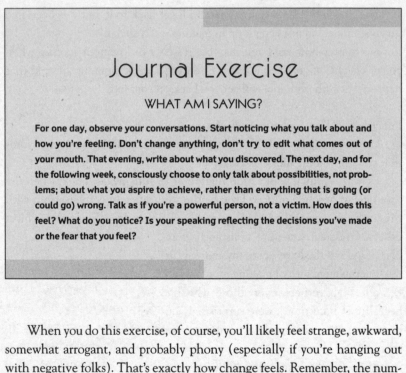

Journal Exercise

WHAT AM I SAYING?

For one day, observe your conversations. Start noticing what you talk about and how you're feeling. Don't change anything, don't try to edit what comes out of your mouth. That evening, write about what you discovered. The next day, and for the following week, consciously choose to only talk about possibilities, not problems; about what you aspire to achieve, rather than everything that is going (or could go) wrong. Talk as if you're a powerful person, not a victim. How does this feel? What do you notice? Is your speaking reflecting the decisions you've made or the fear that you feel?

When you do this exercise, of course, you'll likely feel strange, awkward, somewhat arrogant, and probably phony (especially if you're hanging out with negative folks). That's exactly how change feels. Remember, the number one requirement for success is the willingness to be uncomfortable. Pretty soon, what now feels weird will begin to seem quite normal.

Do the same thing with the conversation going on in your head, the little voices telling you what you can and can't do, urging you to play small, be safe, hold back. Our inner Blanches are by far the worst naysayers we'll ever encounter. Thank them for sharing, and start a new conversation based on what you've learned from this book.

Principle #6—Respect yourself by taking time for you.

We'll never attract people who respect us until we learn to respect ourselves—by taking the time to take care of ourselves.

"I know it sounds selfish, and it's hard to say, but I've got to make me my first priority," financial advisor Katana Abbott told me. "I wasn't taking care of myself, and I got sick for two weeks. I lost my voice. I was exhausted, and I kept ignoring it. I've learned that I have to eat better, exercise, schedule vacations or time off so I can have more energy to better take care of the people I love."

But even more, taking time out is one of the best ways to get in touch with perhaps your most valuable source of support—your Authentic Voice. When you tap into that inner wisdom, you've tapped into a power that's yours forever. And when you claim your power *that's* when the money will follow.

"If I could tell people one thing, it would be to sit down, shut up, and listen to yourself," my friend Linda Moore, a psychologist and author, told me. "We have an inner knowing that is always available. That's the place to start."

One day, Marilyn McCabe Love, a professional speaker and coach, asked herself, "What have I done lately for me?" When her mind hit a blank, she said, "I decided to give myself more time. I took three weeks off work. I read novels, took naps, meditated. I had never taken time for me. I had to learn to sit and be quiet, listen to what was inside me. I found I could hear a choir of voices saying, 'You can do this if you have a vision.' I knew I needed to create a new vision of me as a professional woman who takes herself and her business seriously. I found a whole reservoir within me that said, 'Get up and go.' Then it was 'All right, now one foot in front of the other.' "

In the next four months, Marilyn made $20,000 more than she'd made in the year before. "I took jobs I wanted, turned down the ones that drained me," she exclaimed. "I weaned off old friends, I'm finding new ones. And I am having so much fun."

Journal Exercise

List all the ways you've made time for yourself this past week. Is it enough? If not, what could you do differently?

MOVING ON, SURROUNDED BY SUPPORT. . . .

The word "community" derives from the Latin words *cum munere*, which literally mean to "give among each other." "Giving to yourself" and "receiving from others" are equally critical components for overcoming underearning. Let's carry that thought into the next chapter, to learn what could be the most valuable step you'll ever take for creating a magnificent financial future.

CHAPTER SEVEN HIGHLIGHTS

★ The fourth step, **create a supportive community,** is especially important to underearners who tend to operate in isolation or hang out with naysayers.
★ The people you're with on a regular basis significantly affect your ability to succeed.
★ Four kinds of support are particularly important:
  1. True Believers who cheer you on
  2. Confidantes who you can confide in
  3. Way Showers who model what's possible
  4. Messengers who provide information

★ How do you find supportive people?
1. Realize no one will do this for you, but you don't have to do it alone.
2. Reach out and ask for help.
3. Hang out with the kind of people you want to be like, not who you've been.
4. Recognize the role of the naysayer.
5. Watch what you talk about.
6. Respect yourself by taking time for you.

Conversation with Myself

Who is in your community that you'd like to keep? Did you discover people you'd prefer to spend less time with? How does that feel? Which principle hit home with you? Which one(s) do you need to incorporate more into your life?

EIGHT

Step 5: Respect and Appreciate Money

"More people should learn to tell their dollars where to go instead of asking them where they went."

—*Roger Babson*

"I never wanted to deal with money until I realized that's the only way I'll be able to do what I want to do. What surprises me most is that I enjoy it."

—*Former underearner*

THE GOOD LIFE

There's a big difference between making a good living and enjoying a good life. By way of example, meet Kathy Forbes, a former dental hygienist who now consults for dental practices.

"My husband and I make $100,000 between us," she told me. "But we're living paycheck to paycheck. We just can't get out of debt. What's wrong with this picture?"

Kathy had always assumed the only solution was to work even harder.

But in the workshop she learned otherwise. She went home, doubled her fees, reduced her volunteering, and, indeed, her income rose significantly. Yet she was still so caught up in debt, she couldn't enjoy her success.

She took the workshop a second time and realized what was wrong. She had ignored the final step in her plan to overcome underearning. She had not been respecting and appreciating money. You demonstrate respect and appreciation for money the same way you would anything else of value in your life, be it an heirloom rug, an expensive hand tool, a close friend, or cash in hand. If you want it to last, you've got to take care of it. Throw it around carelessly or ignore it completely and guess what's going to happen?

"When I had extra money, I spent it," Kathy told me. She'd justify going out to dinner with her family because she worked so hard. She bought too much stuff for the house, went to too many movies outside the matinee times, and took way too many short vacations.

"Now I'm spending it to pay off our bills." When we spoke, she'd already reduced her debt to just a few thousand dollars.

"I'm not using credit cards anymore. They're all in the file cabinet. And my husband has agreed to go with me to see a financial counselor. We need a plan for savings and investing."

Remember, my purpose for this book is not just to put a fatter paycheck in your pocket. I want to help you achieve Financial Independence, which means making a good living and enjoying a good life, where money enhances your well-being, not exacerbates your stress. Financial Independence does *not* come from what you earn. It comes from what you *do* with what you have. No matter how sizable your salary, the money will slip through your fingers if you bypass Step Five.

> "Frugality is founded on the principle that all riches have limits."
> —*Edmund Burke*

Sadly, this step is frequently neglected, even by the best and the brightest. It was the biggest surprise I had when interviewing six-figure women. With earnings that ranged anywhere from $100,000 to $7 million, the whopping majority, as confident as they were professionally, were surprisingly insecure financially. They were so busy making money they didn't bother to take care of it.

One middle-aged executive told me, "I feel one step away from a refrigerator carton on the street." She made over $650,000 a year, yet, as she woefully admitted, she had nothing to show for it—no savings, no retirement. "My biggest investments were shoes from Neiman Marcus."

Of all the people I've interviewed for my books, or met during my travels, I can safely say that the ones with the highest net worth were not necessarily the ones who made the most money. They were the ones who took the best care of their money.

Graphic designer Kristen Marie Schuerlein understood the paradox. "I know I'm going to break six figures soon," she said during our interview. "But if I don't work on my behaviors and inner conversations about what stuff I *have* to have, I'll be making $130,000 and still have the same problems I'm having making $65,000." She's right. Like Pavlov's dog salivating when it hears the dinner bell, as soon as people boost their earnings, 'ka-ching,' they bump up their spending, then wonder where those extra bucks went. Kristen knew better. "For me, it's about making conscious choices," she explained, "being very deliberate about what I do with my money."

THE CHOICE IS YOURS

Making conscious, deliberate choices about what you do with your money is precisely what Step Five is all about. And as I see it, there are only four choices you need to make to fully respect and appreciate money. I call these four choices the **Four Rules of Money.**

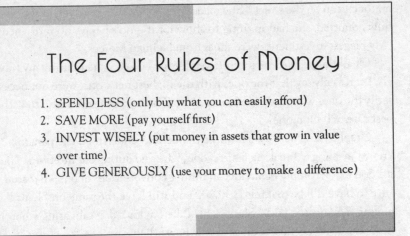

The Four Rules of Money

1. SPEND LESS (only buy what you can easily afford)
2. SAVE MORE (pay yourself first)
3. INVEST WISELY (put money in assets that grow in value over time)
4. GIVE GENEROUSLY (use your money to make a difference)

Most of us have the giving generously part down pat. But unless you handle the first three, giving can become an act of self-sabotage. Not only do you jeopardize your future security, but you diminish the impact you can make with your money.

"My dream is to be a philanthropist," Jody Stevenson, a minister, professional speaker, and life coach, told me during our interview. "But I now know I can't do that until I get my own act together. I can't give away money if I don't have it to give. I see people going into huge debt all the time by tithing to their church. I even used to preach 'Give to God and then everything will fall into place.' I don't believe that anymore. In my former church I'd go 'Don't you dare do that here.' I wish I could go back to all those congregations I spoke to and say, 'Give to yourself first.'"

"That sounds like blasphemy," I gasped.

"I truly believe the act of giving generates abundance, but not if you don't manage your money first, not if you haven't saved anything for yourself or your family."

The success of the fifth step rests in following the Four Rules in the order they're listed. That means, before anything else, don't spend money you don't have. And then make darn sure there's something left over for savings. Believe me, it's next to impossible to overcome underearning if you're still

whipping out credit cards while bills go unpaid. Even if your debts aren't completely paid
off, do *not*—I repeat, DO NOT—add to them.
Not only does debt drain your energy, but it
lulls you into a false sense of sufficiency.

> "The wise man saves for
> the future, but the foolish
> man spends whatever he
> gets."
>
> —*Proverbs 21:20*

"If you use debt to meet your needs, you'll
never be free of underearning," agrees Jerrold
Mundis, author of *Earn What You Deserve*.
"Debt is the cruelest form of poverty. It gives you the illusion that you have
far more than you do."

The Big Must for Overcoming Underearning: Stop Debting Now!

Debt *sucks*. It weighs you down. It drains your energy, your
resources, your peace of mind, and your quality of life. Until
you get rid of your credit cards—tear them up, hide them from
sight, or freeze them in a tin can, taking time to defrost—and
start paying down your bills, you'll have a very tough time
reaching the next level.

BEWARE OF GOING TO EXTREMES

Careless spending or continuing debt is like boarding a train traveling
the wrong way. You'll never get where you want to go. At the same time, you

do *not* want to head in the reverse direction—deprivation, where your emotional and/or physical needs are not being met.

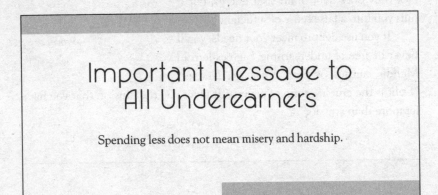

Important Message to All Underearners

Spending less does not mean misery and hardship.

Deprivation is endemic to underearning, being both a symptom and a source of the condition itself. The fifth step does not endorse either scarcity-thinking or severe self-denial. But it does require a certain amount of delayed gratification. There *is* a difference. Cutting back is not the same as cutting out completely. And financial prudence does not imply forsaking necessities, or even some pleasures. The distinction is critical. Discernment's the key.

I'll never forget, years ago, when Karen McCall, founder of the Financial Recovery Institute, explained that by tracking my spending I'd quickly see the quality of life I'd been living. If there's nothing under "personal care" or "entertainment," she told me, you're living in deprivation. Likewise, if you're picking up the tab at every dinner, chances are you're trying to fill a need that lavish spending will never meet.

"When you reduce expenses, don't swing to the opposite extreme," she warned me. "Do it by taking little bits out of each category. Otherwise, budgeting becomes like crash dieting. Deprivation creates a hunger that will drive you right back to the stores on a buying binge." For example, she explained, "if someone had no money for groceries but was getting regular massages, I won't tell them to stop massages. I'd say, 'It looks like massages are important. Let's see how we can build them into a spending program.' "

UNDEREARNERS: START THINKING LIKE A WEALTH BUILDER NOW

For many underearners, life without debt is like dinner without dessert—too big a sacrifice to make. The feeling is, so what's there to look forward to? If this kind of thinking hits close to home, it's time to shift your mind-set from that of a wage earner, consumer, even a bargain hunter to that of a **Wealth Builder.** Wealth Builders make sure their money works as hard for them as they do for it.

"I've had to reframe my whole thinking," the Reverend Jody Stevenson declared. "I realized debt is not a down blanket. It's a drain. The interest you're paying is like buying air. You're spending all this money on nothing. If anything, debt is a messenger. It's a sign you need to change your belief that you're not worthy of financial freedom."

> "I am totally appalled by how much I spent. I allowed myself to spend whatever I wanted. I equated it with nurturing. If I can't buy, I feel a sense of deprivation."
>
> —A self-described "financial bulimic"

"How did you do that?" I asked.

"I stopped debting. I just stopped," she replied matter-of-factly. "I called my credit card people and said, 'What kind of rates are you going to give me? Otherwise I'm going to a lower rate somewhere else.' They marked it way down. Then I transferred what I could into a 2.9 percent interest rate until June. I'm paying it off as fast as I can, and I'm not adding any more."

I was impressed. "Was that difficult for you?"

"I just made some simple changes," she said and laughed, as if she even surprised herself. "I go to used clothes stores now where I get incredible deals on designer outfits. I go to the library for books. I paid cash for all my Christmas presents. I'm working with a bookkeeper, learning to pay attention to every detail. I have a financial advisor, and I've opened a financial freedom account that I put money into every month. I have about $30,000 in there now. It's so exciting to have more money in savings and investments than debt."

Plus, she added, "My income went up $2,500 a month. With no marketing, my coaching practice is full."

Over the years, I've witnessed an inverse correlation between earnings and debt. As *debt goes down, income increases*. And vice versa. Perhaps it's because, as one person explained, "Now that I'm not worrying about how I'll pay my bills, it's like I've freed up all this energy to be so much more creative and strategic in my career."

> "Everyday spending decisions will have a far greater negative impact on one's financial future than any investment decision one can ever make."
>
> —*National Center for Financial Education*

TIME FOR A TWO-PART EXERCISE

Back in Step One, Tell the Truth, I suggested you write down everything you spend. If you haven't done it yet, now's the time.

Even if you're not in debt, even if you've already created a savings cushion, this is a wonderful exercise to get clarity on your finances as well as your quality of life. Your spending patterns reflect your values and priorities. The question is, do you like what you see?

Exercise, Part 1: Track Your Spending

Buy a small notebook that can fit into your pocket or purse. For the next fourteen days to one month, write down every single penny you spend. Whether you pay cash, by check, or by credit card, write down the amount, and what you spend it on. Then come back and fill out the following questions.

How did you feel doing this exercise?

Did you notice any resistance to doing this? (Refer to page 102, the Twelve Signs You're in Resistance. If you found yourself using any of these excuses, it's a sure bet this exercise is important for you to do.)

Did you discover anything you didn't expect?

Were there times you wanted to quit? Did you? Why?

Did you make any changes? What are they?

"The idea of writing everything down is not to spend any differently, but to see where your money goes," says Marcia Brixey, founder of Money Wise Women, a forum for financial education. "However, that's not what people do. They become so aware of overspending that they'll just naturally stop."

If you forget to write some things down, don't let that be an excuse to quit. Just start again and record each expense. You're aiming for persistence, not perfection.

"It took me a few weeks, but I finally kept track of my expenses. I was going to buy something and I said, 'Do I really need that?' It was only $1.70, but hey, it adds up. My Visa balance went down a third since the workshop."

—*Former underearner*

Exercise, Part II:
Spending Review

Create a chart of all your expense categories: mortgage, car, groceries, dining out, entertainment, child care, insurance, and medical. Include categories you might be neglecting, like vacations, clothing, and personal care. Says Karen McCall, "It's just as important to look at where you haven't been spending if it's creating deprivation."

You can do this either by hand or on the computer, using programs like Quicken or Microsoft Money. Record every expenditure, down to the penny, that you've spent in each of these categories. At the same time, record incoming cash, and where it's from. Ask yourself the same five questions that you did in Part I:

How did you feel doing this exercise?

Did you notice any resistance to doing this?

Did you discover anything you didn't expect?

Were there times you wanted to quit? Did you? Why?

Did you make any changes? What are they?

You now have the beginnings of a spending plan. Once you're clear on your cash flow, understand which expenses are fixed (utilities, insurance, etc.), and which you can cut, you can plan your spending for the months to come.

Review this chart to find ways to shave expenses. As the old saw goes, it's easier to find five hundred ways to save $1 than to find one way to save $500.* Whatever extra money you find, immediately put some in savings, the rest into debt payment.

"If you don't create a nest egg," warns Marcia, "then, when something happens, like your car breaking down, you'll be thrown right back into debt."

Tips for Getting Out of Debt

★ Create a spending plan.

★ Stop using credit cards.

★ Talk to your creditors about lowering interest rates.

★ Always pay more than the minimum (otherwise it'll take decades to pay the total).

★ Start paying down the card that has the smallest balance. ("Paying it off faster gives you a sense of accomplishment," says Marcia.)

★ Review your credit report to make sure everything's accurate. (To order a free annual credit report, go to www.annualcreditreport.com, or call 1-877-322-8228.)

★ Get help. Go to a Debtors Anonymous meeting (www.debtors anonymous.org) or contact the Financial Recovery Institute (www.financialrecovery.com).

KRISTEN'S STORY

I found Kristen, the graphic designer we met earlier, an inspiring exam-ple of a Wealth Builder in the making. Her self-described "journey to finan-cial fitness" began with her "spending plan."

"Budget was a bad word," Kristen, thirty-five, told me. "I didn't want to go there. But my goal was to be financially free by age forty. I got from the

---

* See "Ways to Trim Your Spending," by Marcia Brixey, in the appendix.

workshop, in a really powerful way, that financial freedom is *my* responsibility. I sat down and wrote out everything I pay for. This was painful! It hurt just to look at what I was spending. The total was $5,500 a month. Amazing, since I wasn't even making that much! I realized I was living way above my means and I had to start cutting stuff."

> "My advice to you is if you can't afford it, don't buy it."
>
> —*Billionaire Warren Buffett, one of the world's richest men*

Her intention was to live on less but maintain her lifestyle. "I have a very nice lifestyle," she said, laughing. "I didn't think I had a choice when I started this course. I thought this is how much it costs to live. That's it."

When she took a fresh look, she found other options (which is usually what happens—when our intention changes, so does our perception). She refinanced her home, sold her car for a cheaper model, and bought fewer clothes at lower prices, except for occasional splurges. The result?

"I've slashed so much money out of my Kristen overhead," she exclaimed. "I'm still pampering myself by going to the hairdresser and dropping $200 for a cut and color. I wear nice clothes. Yet I'm living on $2,000 less a month than a year ago. And man, do I appreciate things I buy even more! If someone had told me I could do that I'd have told them they were insane."

> "Most financial problems you'll ever face could be avoided if you put aside a part of each paycheck."
>
> —*Susan Alentrod*

In fifteen months, she paid off all her credit card bills and had stopped debting completely. She'd discovered that the best way to stay on budget was to "make financial goals more tempting than current consumption," as my favorite columnist, Jonathan Clements, wrote in the *Wall Street Journal*.

"Budgeting has become a game now," she said enthusiastically. "Let's see how little I can live on and still live well."

Though Kristen admits her income isn't where she wants it to be yet, she's quick to add, "I feel so much more in control of my finances. I'm not panicked that I'll never be financially free. I remember what it was like to be there, and I'm not there anymore."

MAKE YOUR MONEY WORK FOR YOU!

But budgeting was only the beginning. "I've been investing in real estate so I don't have to work, work, work all the time," Kristen said, describing the power of passive income.

"I was a trust fund baby who gave my money to an alleged professional in a very reputable firm and in under two years I'd lost two-thirds of it all," she recalled. "That was the best education I could've gotten. No one cares about my money more than I do. Up until that point, I was so afraid of losing my inheritance, I didn't want to do anything. Now I'm in control instead of acting out of fear and ignorance."

Part of taking control meant addressing her psychological blocks by doing some Inner Work. Often all it takes is a flash of insight, a single "aha," to get us going. That's what happened for Kristen when she did the exercise on page 104, dialoging with herself as a child.

"The big piece for me was seeing myself as a little girl telling me I'll be alone if I'm wealthy. That's what stopped me from taking risks or at least being proactive about my finances," said Kristen. "The investments I made were a direct result of getting that clarity."

Kristen's proactive stance also meant educating herself financially. She continued reading, going to classes, and talking to other investors. She came to understand the *real* meaning of risk.

"Risk is a tricky word," Kristen said. "I'm doing things I would've once called really risky, but now I'm learning and willing to get out of my comfort zone. I've just bought property that I'm fixing up to sell. And I've learned a ton. Now I'm willing to possibly lose some money to make more money."

Ask a financial novice to define "risk," and most will say "losing money." They look at market fluctuations and all they can see is the likelihood of loss. An educated investor, however, sees opportunity for gain.

> "I want to get rich, but I never want to do what there is to get rich."
>
> —*Gertrude Stein*

I learned this years ago, when the smart women I interviewed for my first book gave me essentially the same advice. "You've got to be willing to take some risks in order to make a little extra," said one. "If you put in some time, do a little background work, you can eliminate the worst of it."

In truth, our biggest financial risk is not market volatility. Our biggest risk is to do nothing at all. Sure the market's ups and downs are scary. But you can significantly cut your losses with due diligence, a long-term approach, and adequate diversification. On the other hand, if all your cash is sitting in the bank, or worse, under your mattress, you don't need a crystal ball to predict your future. Your purchasing power will shrink like a bunch of steamed spinach. Unless a portion of your savings is in assets that grow faster than inflation and taxes eat it away, your greatest danger is that you'll outlive your money.

For instance, say you've just gotten a **$1,000** bonus. You're smart enough to save it, so you put it in the bank, where the return is guaranteed and it earns about 2 percent. In about twenty years, your original investment, adjusted for inflation, will be worth a grand total of **$500.** And that's assuming inflation doesn't rise above 3 percent.

But if instead you sent that $1,000 to a stock mutual fund, earning 10 percent, and never add one cent to it, in twenty years you'd be looking at over **$6,000.** Big difference.

What if you don't have $1,000 lying around? Here's the truth: you don't need a lot of money to create wealth, not when you consistently set aside small amounts over a period of time. Mere pocket change adds up surprisingly fast with the magic of compounding (where you're earning interest on your earnings as well as on your original investment). For example, if every day you aside set **50 cents** to put into a mutual fund earning 8 percent (a reasonable return today), in twenty years you'll have **$10,000.**

"I never thought I could invest," a woman declared enthusiastically, "but it's really helped to see I don't need a lot. I've been able to do it with $20 or $50 a week."

Fortunately, she won't find herself in the same position as a sixty-year-old woman I met at a book signing. "I always said I had no money," she told me. "But now that I'm old and I look back on all the money I wasted, I wish to God I had saved more."

I tried to convince her it's never too late to begin, that she'd probably be around at least several more decades. But she wasn't having any part of that.

"I'm scared witless of the market," she told me.

"We always fear what we don't understand," I replied.

FACE IT: YOU HAVE TO EDUCATE YOURSELF

Fear can be a good thing if it forces you to be cautious, to learn the ropes, and to make informed decisions. But fear born from ignorance is crippling. Admittedly, the whole subject of finances can seem truly overwhelming. Who has the time, let alone the interest, to learn a whole new language, to figure out what's a good investment and what's not? It's so much easier to ignore it completely or let someone else do it. That's what I did. Then my husband lost a fortune. And later, when I found an advisor, I got so freaked out when the market crashed in 1987 that I wouldn't listen when he advised me to stay put, generating even more losses.

Today, I'm a huge advocate of hiring financial professionals, be they accountants, lawyers, or advisors. But as I learned the hard way, financial planners make lousy Prince Charmings. No one—I mean *no one*—cares about your money like you do, no matter how trustworthy they may seem.

The First Law of Investing is this:

Never, ever put money in anything you don't understand, whether it's a stock, a bond, or the market itself.

If you ignore the **First Law of Investing,** you put yourself at terrible risk. You don't know what you're buying. You won't understand when to sell. And you have no basis to evaluate advice. Lack of knowledge and poor decisions, more than any down market, is what does most people in. Step 5—respecting and appreciating money—makes sure this won't happen to you.

RIDING THE LEARNING CURVE

I can tell you from experience, it doesn't take a lot of time to get smart about money. And the subject is not nearly as complicated as it seems. What really helped me was to finally understand how the **Learning Curve** works. I devoted a whole chapter to this subject in *Prince Charming Isn't Coming*, which has generated the most interest from readers. Learning anything new, whether it's managing money or speaking Swahili, follows a predictable process of four sequential stages.

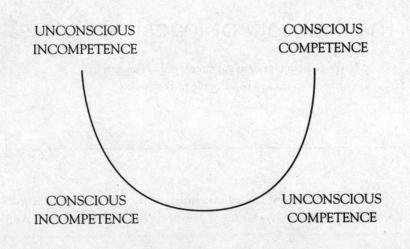

UNCONSCIOUS
INCOMPETENCE

CONSCIOUS
COMPETENCE

CONSCIOUS
INCOMPETENCE

UNCONSCIOUS
COMPETENCE

The Learning Curve

STAGE 1—UNCONSCIOUS INCOMPETENCE. You begin the learning curve knowing nothing. I spent the first forty-five years of my life in this stage. I didn't understand a thing about finance, and frankly I didn't care. I didn't even know what I didn't know. The expression "Ignorance is bliss" pretty much sums up how most of us feel during this stage; why we're perfectly content to remain here forever; and what it usually takes to kick us into the next stage—a crisis!

STAGE 2—CONSCIOUS INCOMPETENCE. As soon as you start seriously studying, whether it's reading *Money* magazine, attending a finance class, or switching on CNBC, you're in the second stage. If the first stage was bliss, this one's a bummer. You're overwhelmed by this "Ohmygawd-I'll-never-understand-this-stuff" feeling. The more you learn, the more baffled you become. Other Stage 2 symptoms include confusion, frustration, anxiety, hopelessness, and apathy.

For some these feelings are short-lived, barely noticeable. But for others, the discomfort is so intense, many bail out. I always did, until I finally didn't. What kept me going was knowing that feeling overwhelmed was a normal, and temporary, part of the learning curve. The key is to continue learning, at whatever pace you can, and eventually you'll get to the next stage.

STAGE 3—UNCONSCIOUS COMPETENCE. The information is slowly sinking in, though you have yet to realize how much progress you've made. But you're starting to get glimpses. A complex issue suddenly makes sense. You can actually read a whole page without fogging up. Someone mentions a mutual

continued

fund and you're actually familiar with it. But these moments are mere hints of what's to come in the final stage.

STAGE 4—CONSCIOUS COMPETENCE. Finally, after weeks, maybe months, of flailing in the dark, you suddenly see light. You can carry on an intelligent conversation and feel reasonably capable of making prudent decisions. There's still more to learn, but you've got a firm grasp on the subject.

In order to complete the process, you must pass through all four stages. Your pace may vary, but the process won't. You may zip through all four stages, get bogged down in one, or move back and forth between several. The secret to finishing the learning curve is to just start, keep going, and never give up.

Journal Exercise

Finish these sentences and write about what came up for you.

I'd love to spend less, but _____.

I'd love to save more, but _____.

I'd love to get out of debt, but _____.

I'd love to invest, but _____.

Can you identify ways to counter the "buts"?

Do you see how the "buts" are merely signs of resistance?

How could you diminish your resistance?

KATHIE'S STORY

"I've known for years I needed to get a handle on finances, but I never did anything about it," Kathie Hightower, fifty, a writer and speaker, told me. Then, in the workshop, she had a string of epiphanies. "I firmly had it in my gut that the only way to make good money was to be in a 'real' profession like law or medicine. And that I'd have to give up my life, kill myself working. That's the way my parents thought," she said. "I didn't even realize how huge that mind-set was, and as long as I had those beliefs I would never make any money. Somehow just seeing that, and how little I was making, there was a lot of anger . . ." Her voice trailed off, then she continued. "So I made a decision to educate myself about finances and see what happens."

What happened was astounding. Her revelations opened the door to a flood of activity.

"I committed to a ninety-day study program. Ninety days seemed manageable. My idea was to immerse myself in it like a college course. Every single day I would read about finances first before anything else. I got a list of books from you, friends, and other financial books. I got a notebook and made notes of my reading. When I didn't understand something, I'd write it down. I kept reading and some of these things came up over and over again. I keep rereading my notes because I don't always get it the first time through.

"Then I started taking proactive steps on some things that had been nibbling in the back of my mind forever. Things I always said, 'I wish Greg would do,' I finally took responsibility for. I made a long list and I'm checking things off.

"I set up a savings account for my business. I did a full inventory of all our household items. I joined an investment club. I am writing down every Visa purchase and subtracting it from my checking account, so when the Visa bill comes, it's not such a huge shock. I had no idea I charged that much. That's been huge—no longer having that fear of opening the bill each month.

"I made an appointment to do wills and health directives, for myself, my husband, and my mother-in-law. When my mother had a stroke and went into a coma, she had everything spelled out, which made it so much easier for my sister and me. I saw how important that was.*

"And I'm not just doing this for my personal side. When I first set up my business, I dove into the whole creativity part without figuring out how to structure it properly. So I took some small business courses. Not that I fully understood them, but I understand more about what I should be doing. I am convinced there are tax advantages and write-offs I'm missing. I made an appointment with an accountant to find out about incorporating my business. And I'm working with someone to make sure my bookkeeping is set up properly. I know this has impacted my earnings."

"How do you feel about all this?" I asked with genuine admiration for her progress. Kathie's response gave me chills. It was an abridged version of the whole process.

"Like I'm an adult," she said, "not waiting for someone to do it for me. It's such a relief, and so empowering."

---

* Months later, Kathie e-mailed me: "My mother-in-law died suddenly and very unexpectedly in January of this year. My husband and sister-in-law are still thanking me for taking the initiative and convincing her of the importance of getting everything up to date with her will last year."

The Money
Appreciation Guide

Check the statements that are true for you.

☐ I am clear on my financial goals.
    They are:

☐ I know my net worth
    It is:

☐ I have no credit card debt.
    If I do, the total is:

☐ I have enough savings to live on for three to six months.
    The amount is:

☐ I have money invested in a retirement account.
    How much:
    It is invested in:

☐ I have investments outside a retirement account.
    They are:

☐ I understand the investments I own.

☐ I will have enough money to live on in retirement.

☐ I have a will.

☐ I know where all my financial documents and records are.

    This is what respect and appreciation of money looks like.

    Pay special attention to the statements you did not check—that's the work you need to do next.

CHAPTER EIGHT HIGHLIGHTS

★ The fifth step, **respect and appreciate money,** ensures that you make a good living *and* enjoy a good life.

★ It's critical to take care of your finances by following the Four Rules of Money: Spend Less, Save More, Invest Wisely, and Give Generously . . . in that order.

★ Above all, you must stop debting and start paying off your credit cards.

★ Cutting back doesn't mean cutting out buying completely. Instead, track your expenses, do a spending plan, and educate yourself financially.

★ Getting smart about money requires traveling through the four phases of the Learning Curve (Unconscious Incompetence; Conscious Incompetence; Unconscious Competence; Conscious Competence).

★ The First Law of Investing: never put money in anything you don't understand.

★ Your biggest risk is *not* market volatility, but making uninformed choices or doing nothing at all.

Conversation With Myself

How did you feel reading this chapter? Were there any surprises? Did anything disturb you? On a scale of 1 to 10, how would you rate yourself as a Wealth Builder? What will you do differently? Has the Inner Work you've been doing affected your relationship to the Four Rules of Money?

Ensuring Success

> *"Don't let who you are get in the way of what you might become."*
>
> —*Source unknown*

> *"Pray for potatoes with a hoe in your hand."*
>
> —*Irish proverb*

NINE

Call to Action

"Action and becoming are one."

—*Meister Eckhardt*

YOUR GAME PLAN

There's a story about a snail climbing a cherry tree in the middle of winter. A beetle looks down, spies the snail slowly inching up the frozen bark, and cries out, "There ain't no cherries up here." Unfazed, the snail replies, "There will be by the time I get there."

That little snail is a stellar example of the **Recommended Game Plan for Overcoming Underearning.** *Think big. Act small. And never, ever stop until you attain your goal, no matter what.* I heard variations of this mantra from everyone I interviewed who set their sights high and eventually reached them.

"As long as I'm facing the right direction, it doesn't matter the size of my steps."

—*Erica Jong*

Kathleen White came to the workshop after being laid off. She was determined to find an even higher-paying job, even though everyone swore she'd have to settle for less. Within eight months, Kathleen had landed a job in senior management making more money.

"There are always going to be people who will try to veer you off your path," she told me during our interview. "I just kept saying, 'That's not true.' I was extremely focused on the amount of money I wanted to make, and, of course, I set a very high goal from where I was."

She left our class, and like the snail, kept plodding away, relentlessly focused on her goal, doing whatever she could to move ahead. She listened to motivational tapes, repeated daily affirmations "about the good things that would happen," and exercised five times a week for thirty minutes because "that's all the time I could spare." She forced herself to network, to ask for referrals, and "tried to only be around positive people." And always, she said, "I felt the fear and acted anyway."

> "It is by tiny steps we as-
> cend to the stars."
>
> —*Jack Ludstrom*

When I asked what advice she'd give others, her reply neatly summed up the Outer Work of underearning: "*You have to keep at it every day. It's basically a way of life.*"

Overcoming underearning doesn't happen overnight. It's a gradual process of faithfully following the Five-Step Plan until it becomes a way of life.

1. Tell the truth about what's not working, and what is.
2. Make a firm decision about what you truly want.
3. Look for opportunities to stretch by doing what you think you can't do.
4. Surround yourself with a supportive community.
5. Respect and appreciate money by taking good care of it.

These steps are not something you can read about and forget. You really must make them part of your daily routine, because if you do something every day, no matter how small, no matter how brief, you will eventually arrive at your destination.

When I asked Realtor Donna Weaver to explain her dramatic increase in earnings, she replied without delay, "I do something daily. Knowing I can take small steps to accomplish small things allows me to take bigger steps to accomplish bigger things."

Likewise, entrepreneur Laurie Lamoureux told me, "I got through this quagmire of financial avoidance just by forcing myself to take little baby steps every day."

Speaking coach Jean Hamilton, who regularly hit the monthly financial goals she'd set for herself in a weekly ledger, said the same. "I just took it one step at a time. There were times I found myself not doing something because I was scared, but you build up all this fear, and every single time the fear beforehand is worse than actually doing the thing."

"That which we persist in doing becomes easier—not because the nature of the task has changed, but our ability to do it has increased."

—Ralph Waldo Emerson

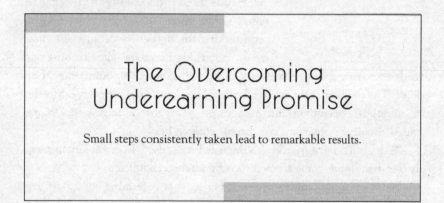

The Overcoming Underearning Promise

Small steps consistently taken lead to remarkable results.

Small steps are critical for overcoming underearning. They dilute the fear, minimize the discomfort, and shrink what may at first seem daunting down to feeling doable. But *consistency is the key for creating miracles*.

MAKING FINANCIAL SUCCESS A HABIT

Author John Steinbeck once wisely observed, "In writing, habit seems to be a much stronger force than willpower or inspiration." The same could be said about earning.

Look at the ten traits of underearners on page 31, especially the ones that apply to you. Can you see how these traits are the result of and have been reinforced by your recurring thoughts and repetitive behaviors? You acquired them early, strengthened them continually, and assimilated them so thoroughly that they became an integral part of who you are, without ever questioning their value to your life.

> "Thoughts become words. Words become actions. Actions become habits. Habits become character. Character becomes destiny."
>
> —*Source unknown*

Habits aren't necessarily bad. They're nature's time-savers, allowing us to act without thinking through every detail every time we do something mundane like brushing our teeth or paying a bill. Sometimes those habits serve us. Sometimes they don't. The problem is we rarely take the time to note the difference. Mostly, we mindlessly operate on unconscious programs that were installed in our brains, usually by observing our parents early in life.

"I've always been in debt. It's the way I was raised. Everyone in my family had debt. It felt comfortable," Jody Stephenson admitted.

But it's not our family's patterns, per se, that determine our habits. It's the unconscious decisions *we* made about them. Like the two sisters, one a drunk, the other a teetotaler. When asked why they turned out the way they did, both had the same response: "Because my parents were alcoholics." We spend our lives imitating or rebelling against what we saw growing up.

> "Any financial dysfunction is a defective view of and appreciation for oneself coupled with unworkable learned behavior."
>
> —*George Moore,*
> And Forgive Us Our Debts

A wealthy woman once confided in me, "My mother was always in debt. We made do with so little. I vowed I'd never live like that."

While another, a chronic underearner, explained, "I've patterned my life on my mother's angst: there's never enough." And a struggling filmmaker with a successful father declared, "I know what fiscal responsibility looks like and it's boring, really boring. That's not how I want to live."

> "Men's natures are alike. It is their habits that separate them."
>
> —Confucius

Much of the work we've done throughout this book has been to uncover the early decisions you made about yourself and money. Those decisions sprouted, unchallenged, into deep-seated beliefs, giving birth to the habits that have gotten you where you are today. Trying to change habits without doing the Inner Work is akin to defying gravity, so intense is habit's invisible pull. That's why I've placed so much emphasis on self-awareness.

Combine the Outer Work with the Inner Work, and you can efficiently replace old habits with new ones. But it takes conscious, forced repetition on a regular basis. That's how the Recommended Game Plan for Overcoming Underearning works.

"I came from a blue-collar background," social worker Janey Cook told me. "My mother was a telephone operator. You never thought about making money. You just did your job. This workshop got me thinking differently."

Thinking differently, in my experience, inevitably spurs us to act differently, too. I saw it over and over again in the Doers like Janey.

"I started building new habits by being more conscious," she said. "I would do something every day for at least fifteen minutes. It may be just reading an article, balancing my checkbook, seeing how much clients owe me, or taking bills out and putting them in a pile. I've already made saving for retirement a habit. I put away fifteen percent of everything that comes in."

Still, Janey admitted, "some days I get tired of doing stuff, but I won't let myself give up. I'd be giving up on myself if I did. No, I've made this a daily practice."

The point is to make the new behaviors such an integral part of your life that when ignored, you feel like something is missing. Actions that seem uncomfortable in the beginning will eventually become even more uncomfortable *not* to do.

Creating the Habit of Respecting Money

When I was trying to get smart about money, I devised a plan for myself that was amazingly effective at changing my habitual avoidance. Others who've done it have said the same. Try it for three months, and see if you don't become a whole lot smarter about taking care of money.

1. EVERY DAY, READ SOMETHING ABOUT MONEY, even if it's just for a minute or two, even if it's only the headlines of the business section of the newspaper, or a *Money* magazine while you're waiting in line at the grocery. I remember subscribing to the *Wall Street Journal*, but I never read it because I couldn't understand it. So I'd lay Section C, about investing, on the kitchen counter and every day I'd walk by it, figuring by osmosis I'd pick something up. That was the smartest thing I could've done. To this day, if I do nothing else, I'll glance at the headlines in Section C. So much of getting smart or smarter about money is understanding the jargon, the terminology, the current trends. You can do the same with financial programs on TV or the radio. "I always turn on the news while I cook dinner," a woman told me. "Now, instead of local murders, I watch the nightly PBS business report."

2. EVERY WEEK, HAVE A CONVERSATION ABOUT MONEY. It's amazing how willing people are to discuss money, and how much you can learn from them. I truly believe secrecy and silence keeps you stuck. I discovered this from my interviews with financially savvy women. Whenever you meet anyone who knows more than you, take advantage of the opportunity. Ask people how they got smart, the mistakes they made, and what's worked best for them. Take finance classes at local colleges, adult education centers, and from most brokerage firms. (Sure they want to sell you something, but don't dismiss them. They're free, you don't have to buy anything, you'll meet others like yourself, and I always learned a tremendous amount from them.) Also talk to your friends. When I did, we formed an investment club, a fabulous way to have fun learning by doing.

3. EVERY MONTH, SAVE. Automatically have money transferred from your checking account or paycheck to your savings account or money market fund. It doesn't matter how much, even $5 a month is great. What if you don't have anything left over at the end of the month? Go back to the two-part exercise in chapter 8 and find ways to trim your expenses. Or give up something small, like that cookie after work and bank or collect the savings. One woman told me that when her grandson was born she quit smoking, and put the money she would have spent on cigarettes into mutual funds. Three years later, she had $10,000 for her grandson's education. Another gave up drinking Coke, put that money into Coca-Cola stock, and bought her first condo with the profits. Still another funded her IRA with loose change from her purse, coins she found in pockets doing laundry, and cash from the coupons she redeemed at the market.

CLOSING RITUALS

At this point in my workshop, we come to what I call the closing rituals. These are a series of exercises designed to create daily rituals for turning the Five Steps into favorable habits, and to craft an action plan that you can routinely update. Let us do the same. We'll start by declaring your goal.

"By design or neglect, Americans have tucked away loose change to the tune of an estimated $7.7 billion, enough to pay for the war in Afghanistan for nearly eight months."

—*Associated Press report appearing in the* Seattle Times, *February 24, 2002*

My Earnings Goal

First, based on how you feel now, fill in the box below. Then refer to this same exercise on page 93. Did your vision change?

THIS YEAR I WILL MAKE $ _____ **.**

Next, you're going to identify what you need to do to reach this goal. You'll be adding to this list every week.

Exercise: My Next Steps

Check off the action steps listed below that you're willing to do. These are just to give you ideas. There's space to come up with your own.

- ☐ Write down my intentions.
- ☐ Observe my attitudes, beliefs, thoughts, feelings, and choices around money.
- ☐ Do daily affirmations.
- ☐ Determine what I need to let go of.
- ☐ Feel the fear and go for it anyway.
- ☐ Raise my fees; ask for a raise.
- ☐ Think bigger, bigger, BIGGER!
- ☐ Embrace my BITCH.
- ☐ Read something about money.
- ☐ Negotiate bonuses, stock options, vacation time, commuting expenses, flextime, early salary review, etc.
- ☐ Act as if I'm worth it.*
- ☐ Read inspirational books. (See "Recommended Resources" in the appendix.)
- ☐ Talk about money with someone who knows more than me.
- ☐ Be direct and ask for what I want.
- ☐ Ask for more responsibility and challenges.
- ☐ Do something that makes me uncomfortable.
- ☐ Look for the gift in my problems.
- ☐ Assemble my support community.
- ☐ Hire a coach.
- ☐ Find a financial advisor.
- ☐ Join a professional network.
- ☐ Spend less than I earn.*
- ☐ Stop using credit cards and pay for everything with cash.
- ☐ Set up a debt-repayment plan with my creditors or transfer balances to a lower-interest credit card.
- ☐ Get clarity by writing down everything I spend.
- ☐ Pay myself first by having $___ automatically withdrawn from my bank account monthly.
- ☐ Write about money in my journal.
- ☐ Other:
- ☐ Other:
- ☐ Other:

* Required.

Now transfer the steps you checked on page 177 to the contract below. Tell at least one person what you've decided to do because you'll need a witness, as well as a watchdog.

Exercise: Contract with Myself

Sign the contract below, listing at least five of the activities you checked above. Add five more each week. Ask your buddy to witness your signature and set up a check-in time, preferably weekly.

I, _____, do hereby commit to make overcoming underearning a pressing priority. Every day, for thirty days, I will spend some time doing something on this list. Here's what I will do:

Day 1 _____	11 _____	21 _____
2 _____	12 _____	22 _____
3 _____	13 _____	23 _____
4 _____	14 _____	24 _____
5 _____	15 _____	25 _____
6 _____	16 _____	26 _____
7 _____	17 _____	27 _____
8 _____	18 _____	28 _____
9 _____	19 _____	29 _____
10 _____	20 _____	30 _____

Signed _____   Date _____

Witness _____   Date _____

The next exercise, the Daily Do-It, is the most important part of this thirty-day commitment. Whenever you slip up, start again where you left off. If something feels uncomfortable, as it surely will, keep going. Remember, any time you do something different, it's going to feel awkward, weird, not right, and you'll instinctively want to go back to the old way. Keep in mind, the number one requirement for overcoming underearning is to feel the discomfort and do it anyway.

Exercise: Daily Do-It

There are three parts to this daily ritual—commitment, action, reflection.

1. COMMITMENT. Each day decide what you're going to do on the list.
2. ACTION. Do it.
3. REFLECTION. Think about what you did or didn't do.

If you did what you committed to, reflect on what you learned, how the experience was, and what you will do the next day. If you didn't do it, ask yourself why and use your response as information. I've found that analyzing why you didn't do something to be the most helpful part of the exercise. Mull over the answer, write about it in your journal, discuss it with a friend. The point is not to judge or berate your lack of action, but to get insight into your resistance. Uncovering the root of your resistance will dramatically expedite the process.

Repeat the ritual the next day. At least once a week, check in with your buddy.

Finally, this last exercise is meant to help you clear out whatever may be holding you back, keeping you stuck, or getting in the way of your getting ahead. This can be a very powerful ritual if you approach it thoughtfully and intentionally.

Exercise: Letting Go

Look at the My Letting-Go List you made on page 121. Is there anything you want to add?

Are you ready to let go of what's on that list? Are you *really* ready? If there are things you're not ready to release, that's absolutely fine. The point is to tell the truth and make a conscious choice. You can always choose to let them go at a later date. This exercise should be repeated monthly.

Take a sheet of paper, cut it into strips, and on a each strip, write what you're ready to let go of. You are going to rip up each item one by one. But as you do, talk to whatever it is you're giving up: thank it for how it once served you but no longer does; ask if it has anything to tell you; say what else needs to be said, and then tell it goodbye.

Now throw away—or better yet, burn—the paper.

These final exercises are not meant to be one-shot experiences. Doing these rituals regularly will assure that the fruit of your labor is within reach when you arrive at the next level. And it won't just be more money you'll find. You'll discover you have the power to create the life of your dreams—one step at a time.

As we near the conclusion of this book, and all the work we've done together, let us stop and consider the words of a Buddhist sage, Chig Yam Trungpa: "*If you begin, go all the way. If you begin and quit, the unfinished business you left behind begins to haunt you all the time.*" Don't allow yourself to be plagued by what could have been. Do a little something every day toward your goal and never, ever stop until you reach your destination, no matter what. You owe it to yourself, and as you're about to see in the next chapter, you won't be the only one who profits.

CHAPTER NINE HIGHLIGHTS

★ The Recommended Game Plan for Overcoming Underearning is this: think big; act small; and never, ever give up.

★ Small steps *consistently* taken will take you to the next level in earnings.

★ The whole point is to turn the Five Steps into habitual behaviors by practicing them daily.

Conversation with Myself

Can you see how your habits have gotten you to this point? What new behaviors would you rather be displaying? On a 1 to 10 scale, how committed are you to this thirty-day program? If your commitment level is below 10, why? What could possibly get in the way of your overcoming underearning? Looking back at what you've read, how would you sum up the most important points you've learned?

"There are costs and risks to a program of action. But they are far less than the long-range risks and costs of comfortable inaction."

—*John F. Kennedy*

Putting It All Together: Tami's Story

*"When I left the workshop, I remember
going down in the elevator thinking, "Why didn't
anyone tell me this twenty years ago?
How different my life would've been."*

—*Tami Mathisen*

I'd like to leave you with a true story that embodies much of what I've written about in these pages. May Tami's tale strengthen your commitment to overcome underearning and inspire you to spread the word. When you turn this Five-Step Plan into a daily practice, you become a testimony to others that there *is* a better way.

IN THE BEGINNING . . .

Tami Mathisen was a heavy-set, thirty-eight-year-old woman who wore black-rimmed glasses and long hair swept back into a pony tail. She came to my Overcoming Underearning™ workshop for the same reason most people do—she was geared up to go to the next level, but didn't know how to get there.

"I was tired of struggling so hard, tired of having so little, and really tired of always needing to scale back," she told me. "I wanted to retrieve my life. I wanted more for my daughter."

Tami had hit rock bottom, physically and financially.

"I'd been very ill for years—several major surgeries. Our income went down to nothing. So did our quality of life. We had to make major adjustments, scale way back. After being ill, I knew I couldn't keep working this hard and have so little." She added, with a sigh, "When what you want seems so far away, you wonder if it's even worth it to try. But the timing of the workshop was perfect. I was feeling good for the first time in fifteen years."

Feeling Stuck?

Timing is everything. If you're experiencing difficulty overcoming underearning, perhaps you're not quite ready. Perhaps more pressing issues, such as the ones below, need to be addressed first. If you suspect that's the case, I highly recommend personal counseling.

★ Health issues
★ Relationship problems
★ Lack of priority or motivation
★ Your comfort motive is stronger than your profit motive
★ Absence of the Click (knowing you're worth it)

Tami and her husband own a Seattle-area landscape maintenance firm, which suffered terribly during Tami's illness. Once she was healthy, she was back helping her husband. She had also started a holiday crafts business, hoping to further boost the family's income.

Still, her finances were floundering. "I had read lots of books about money but nothing helped."

TRUTH CLEARS THE WAY

"I never realized how many of the things I thought about money were wrong," Tami exclaimed during our interview after the workshop. "Like I thought all wealthy people were greedy, and that it was bad to want money."

(*Tami is about to explain the value of doing this work with other people.*) "Part of it was sitting in that room with all those other women who had what I considered very respectable jobs. We came from different backgrounds, different generations, but they were struggling with the same things I'd struggled with. They were feeling the same way I was. I saw it didn't matter if you were making $3 an hour or $300 an hour. You could climb as high as you wanted. No one could stop you. (*Tami starts with Step 1, Tell the Truth.*)

"When we did the ceiling exercise—where you had to close your eyes and write how you'd feel making different amounts of money—I was stunned that I stopped at a certain point and couldn't go any further. (*The Inner Work immediately opens her eyes.*) The idea that you set your own ceiling because of the worth you place on yourself, that you limit yourself just by how you feel, was astounding. I never believed that I could have more than just enough to support myself. Suddenly, my vision grew. I thought, 'You know, what if I did make $250,000?' I began to feel like money wasn't such a big insurmountable thing after all."

(*Telling the truth also means acknowledging your strengths.*) "I always knew that I was terrible with money because my mother told me I was. She'd always say, 'Why should I give you an allowance when you're so bad with money, and you'll blow it on something stupid anyway.'

"The truth was that part of the reason I wasn't managing money well was because I didn't give myself credit for the money I *was* managing. Sitting in the workshop, I saw all these other women who had corporate jobs and huge incomes who couldn't manage their money either. I had done a lot better job than I had given myself credit for.

"I realized maybe I'm not as bad as I thought. I had home-schooled my daughter, run the house, done the budget, managed my husband's company, and this twelfth-grade dropout taught herself how to do payroll! So maybe I wasn't as bad at business as I thought I was. Once I gave myself credit, instead of focusing on what I did wrong, something clicked. My work was worth more because I was worth more." (*There is that important Click.*)

Her husband, Terry, saw the change in his wife immediately. He, too, was affected.

"She came home all motivated and excited. The workshop empowered her, gave her more ambition," he told me, admitting "I'm not fast to accept stuff. It takes me a while to get in the mode. But I liked the things she was saying. It was like there was a new world of opportunity out there."

Terry recalled his own background. "The only thing I learned about money was from my parents. And they weren't a great example. I never really knew there was another way."

DIVING INTO THE DISCOMFORT ZONE

Tami immediately realized she had to make some changes. (*She begins Step 2 with firm decisions.*) One was to discontinue her crafts business. "I was putting way too much time into something that wasn't going to generate the income we needed," she said.

The other move was to "completely restructure" the landscaping firm. "I knew my husband had to make changes in the way that we do business, ASAP." (*She dives into Step 3, the Stretch.*)

Tami's first change created a huge fight. "I came home from the workshop and added $12 an hour onto my husband's billing, which increased our revenue almost thirty percent," she recalled. However, when she informed Terry of the price hike, "he stormed out of the house and was gone for a while."* She wasn't surprised by his reaction. "He always felt that it is so ungrateful not to be thankful for the work he had. He felt raising his prices was greedy, that people were going to drop us, we'd lose all our business. But I had to take the risk. Even if twenty percent left, we'd still make more money."

(*The inevitable resistance shows up.*) "I wasn't so much mad," Terry explained. "I was more scared than anything. Raising prices was not something

---

* Author's note: Okay, *maybe* she should not have made a unilateral decision, but at least she took action!

I felt comfortable doing. My parents taught me to do everything on the safe side. If it wasn't safe, you'd better not do it.

"But Tami was insistent," her husband said. "I think she felt better about herself and was ready to take the risk, and if we lost customers, so be it.

"Each time we went to the mailbox, I'd think, 'How many pissed-off clients am I going to lose today?' And you know what? No one said anything. We haven't lost any customers. And new ones just say, 'Well, fine,' to the price. That opened me up a lot.

(*Here comes his Click.*) "I saw my customers valued my services more than I did. I feel like I'm worth more than I ever thought before. I've decided that I'm going to charge this price and stick to my guns. If I get it, I get it. If I don't, I don't. That's a real big change for me. I realize if you don't take a risk, how will you make money?

"Before, in the wintertime," Terry continued, "I'd have to take lower-paying jobs. Not this year. We figured out how to have a stable income even in a seasonal business. We put all our customers on yearly contracts so we have income that is the same year-round."

Terry also stopped bartering (*classic symptom of underearning*), refusing to do anything for free. "We upped our income $22,000 in just the first few months," said Tami. And Terry added, "I'm a lot less stressed."

Raising prices wasn't the only big change Tami made. (*We're about to see how change in one area affects other areas as well.*)

"Within two weeks after the workshop," she told me, "I met with a banker and an architect. We live in a mobile home, which will be gone soon. We're building a new house. And I bought a brand-new car. I never would've done that before, because in my family, owning a new car was considered selfish and greedy. In fact, someone from my family just said to me, 'Who are you to own a new car?' " (*The ubiquitous Angel of Gloom.*)

"I paid for it with my own money. I even worked the loan down to 6½ percent. I had no credit in my name. I had always done it in my husband's name," she said proudly. (*Tami was smart. Every woman should establish credit for herself, and pay it off promptly.*)

Again, her husband was upset. "But it wasn't the car, or the house," Tami acknowledged. "It was the changes we were going through."

Terry agreed. "She was breaking the mold, and I didn't know if I liked it."

Tami didn't want to lose her husband. But she wasn't about to sacrifice her goals to placate his fears. (*Respecting one's own needs doesn't mean deserting another.*) Her solution: "I made Terry do the Overcoming Underearning™ workbook. I told him, 'The train is leaving the station. You can get on in the front or the back, but if you miss it, the train's gone.'" Terry went through the workbook with his wife, albeit begrudgingly at first.

"It totally changed him," Tami exclaimed. "Neither one of us had ever looked at money in our lives. You just earned and spent. We had to learn to use money as a tool." Enlightenment, however, is not without emotional consequences.

THE EMOTIONAL BACKLASH

"For my husband," Tami recalled, "the sentence completion [*the Digging Down to the Roots exercise*] was really difficult to do. He was raised to respect his family. If he changed how he felt about money, he felt it was a betrayal to his father. It took him a week to do it."

Tami, too, experienced her own repercussions. (*She comes to the dark side of self-determination.*) "The hardest thing for me," she said, "was accepting I had spent my whole life undercutting myself. It was very emotional. It made me very angry at myself. At age twenty-one I had a corporate job, making $65,000. I had an expense account, a driver, and my mom called me 'highfalutin.' My uncle was wealthy, and she always resented him. So she made me feel like wealthy people were bad, and it was wrong to have more money than you need. I chose not to do what I wanted, because it felt greedy, and I felt horrible about having too much money." The pain in her voice was audible when she added with a deep sigh, "I went into the Peace Corps because it was humbler."

BUILDING COMMUNITY

It's no surprise that Tami doesn't see as much of her mother these days. "It's difficult to talk to my mom about this. She's on my 'naysavers list' so I am not with her as much." (*Tami's at Step Four, Create a Supportive Community.*) "In fact, we've limited the time we spend with our whole family, who always gripe about money. We didn't do Christmas with them this year.

"We've totally changed our circle of friends. I never realized how much we complained about people with money until I started paying attention to the people around me. We stopped being with anyone who was negative. I won't have them over. If we are going to change our life around money, we have to be careful who we spend time with. I know what people say to me is very powerful.

"We screen our clients. If they're worried about cost, I refer them. I only take people who want things done right, with quality.

"We stopped going to our church, because it has a major money dysfunction.

"I dropped a lot of social responsibilities, so I have more time."

Tami and Terry have replaced these negative influences with a wonderful new habit they've begun with their fifteen-year-old daughter. "Now we have family meetings, and we talk about money which we never did before." (*Your spouse and children are a critical component of a supportive community.*)

TAKING GOOD CARE OF MONEY

Neither Tami nor her family had ever thought about financial goals. (*Together they do Step 5, Respect and Appreciate Money.*) "I started reading a lot of books," she told me. "I went to the Money Wise Women Forum. I pay close attention to when the money comes in and where it goes out. I'm doing expense reports, and every Sunday at family meetings, my husband and daughter both get a copy so they can see where we are as far as budget for the month. It's made them really conscious of what we're spending.

"Before, if my husband needed something, like a new mower, he'd come to me and I'd have to figure out how to do it. Now he has to fill out an expense report and put it into a priority category. If it's not in by Friday, he doesn't get the cash." (*Setting boundaries is important for overcoming underearning. It's the only way out of codependence.*)

"We're even buying groceries totally differently. Before we just bought what we wanted. Now we only buy what we need—and we make sure there's enough money to pay for it."

(*She's following the Four Rules of Money in the right order: Spend Less, Save More, Invest Wisely, Give Generously.*) "All three of us made an agreement that we wouldn't spend any extra money that came in right away, but journal about it and wait for two weeks. Then, at the end of two weeks, we'd ask in family meetings, is this what we want to do? For example, we thought about going to the aquarium. Two weeks later, the answer was no. It was an exercise in impulsiveness. But my daughter and I did decide to go to the Space Needle in Seattle for lunch. We'd never been there before. We thought it would be ridiculously expensive. It wasn't. And sitting up there, the city looked so small and I felt so empowered." (*Cutting back doesn't mean cutting out.*)

"Because we've paid attention to our budget, and stopped investing in the crafts company that wasn't going anywhere, we had accumulated $2,000 extra we used for a trip to Mexico."

"We're all a lot more conscious of how we are spending," Terry concurred. "And I'm starting to think about money for the long term. How can we get the most out of the money we are making?"

His wife couldn't be happier. "Terry's on the Internet now, looking for home foreclosures," she declared jubilantly. "This is humongous. The whole idea of investing was a revelation for him. One day, he said to me, 'You know, if we're really good with our money, and we invest it well and make it work for us, we won't have to work so hard.' I had to walk over and put my hand on his forehead and say, 'Are you feeling all right?'

"Even though I knew we needed to do things differently with our money, I just didn't know how I could get him to come along with me. To have him *ahead* of me in enthusiasm is so exciting."

Terry was indeed enthusiastic. (*Terry shows us how the steps overlap. In this instance, he's using community support to help him better respect money.*)

"I've started reading more about investing. I'm talking to customers who invest, asking a lot of questions. I've never ever talked to people about money before. But you know, you can learn a lot from others. I've got a sense now of what the power of money can do."

And both are acting on that sense. The Mathisens had just gone to a foreclosure auction where they saw "a tiny little lot for $4,000," Tami said. "I went to the man who lived next door to it and asked if he would buy it. He said, 'Sure, I'd love it,' and agreed to pay $34,000. The next day I went back to the auction, wrote a check for $4,000, and quick-deeded it to him an hour later. He was thrilled." So were they. But the Mathisens both warned me, "You have to be really careful with foreclosures. We did *a lot* of research beforehand." (*The First Law of Investing: never buy anything you don't understand.*)

THE OVERCOMING UNDEREARNING GAME PLAN

"I keep your workbook by my desk and refer to it all the time," said Tami. "I did everything on the Contract with Myself. It was very important to me. It was the first time I ever made a contract with myself and I knew I didn't want to let myself down."

She looked at her list and gave me examples. (*Lots of small consistent steps created her remarkable results.*)

"I put down 'Be direct and ask for what you want.' That was fun. In our family, we hinted. Now if we want something, a new pair of shoes or to go camping, we post it on the fridge. It seemed so selfish at first. I always made sure everyone had something but me. Now I ask for it. In April, I wrote, 'I want to go back to school.' And a month later, I did it.

"I have my 'stretch' posted: 'Do the Unfamiliar.' I applied it to school. I took classes I knew nothing about, and it was a heavy load.

"I wrote, 'Think Bigger,' and put it on the fridge. That was my biggest limit. I never ever thought to think bigger. I also have my list of Way Showers on my bulletin board, and I keep adding to them. I just finished crossing off the last naysayer.

"We also post the twelve signs of resistance. We catch ourselves using them all the time. My daughter keeps them in her locker, and her teachers tell her to look there every time she makes an excuse."

In addition, Tami wrote on her contract, "Remove anything in my life that will get in the way of living my dream." By the time of our last interview, she had lost over fifty-five pounds (*weight loss is a frequent by-product of the increased self-esteem that comes from following the Five Steps*). "I stopped putting garbage in my mouth and ate healthy." That's not the only garbage Tami got rid of. (*There is enormous power in letting go!*)

"After the workshop, we purged everything—every drawer, cupboard, storage. We had a garage sale, drove truckloads of stuff to Habitat for Humanity and the dump. How could I know how much money I needed in my life if I didn't know what I had?"

Again, Terry balked. "At first I wasn't excited about getting rid of so much. I always felt like if I had more stuff, I had more wealth. My grandmother was like that. So were my parents. Now I like not having clutter. I know what I have, and I don't feel so driven to buy stuff."

"The clarity is empowering," Tami declared. "It's like 'This is who we are; this is what we have; this is what we want; here's how we get from "want" to "have."'"

THE VIEW FROM THE TOP
OF THE CHERRY TREE

Tami's the first to admit, "It's hard work. There were days I didn't want to do this stuff." (*Here she shows us the value of journaling.*) "But I keep journals, and I'll go back to them and I'll see how I'm changing, not just about money but everything. I look different. I dress differently. My hair's different. My marriage is different. There's a sense of calm, security, and mutual respect between us that wasn't there before."

Then Tami, her hair attractively styled in short layers, added with a wide grin, "The very best part for me is that I'm impressed with myself. I went to the workshop thinking I needed to learn my earning potential. I came out knowing I had everything I needed the whole time. But I had to live it every day." (*Sticking with the process, making it a way of life, not only eliminates underearning but keeps strengthening our self-esteem.*)

CHANGE YOURSELF, CHANGE THE WORLD

(*We're about to see what I believe is one of the responsibilities as well as rewards of overcoming underearning—helping others.*) "I not only had the chance to change me, but to affect my daughter's life as well," Tami said proudly. "She's gotten smarter just by watching us. She thinks more about what she buys. She'll go to the library instead of buying books, and then puts that money in her savings account.

"And for the first time, my husband realizes that life can be more than just getting by, that there's retirement, that he doesn't have to work until he dies."

"I was going through life numb," Terry confessed. "I don't feel numb anymore. I feel energized. I have more self-confidence."

I asked Tami how she would sum up her experience. She responded by recounting an incident that occurred earlier in the week while shopping for clothes. She started chatting with the saleswoman, and learned she was twenty-five years old, taking home $5 an hour, living in subsidized housing, struggling to support four kids.

"What are you doing here?" Tami asked her incredulously. "You have a degree in office technology!"

"It's what I've always done," the young woman sighed. "It's easy."

Tami looked her straight in the eye and declared firmly, "This is *not* the best you can do." Then she helped the young woman come up with a list of next steps.

> If you grow your money so you have more than you need, that's wealth. If you use your money to make a difference, that's power.

A week later, the sales clerk called Tami, full of gratitude. "I feel like an angel just landed in my life and told me I was accepting where I was and I didn't have to do that," she said.

"I told her what I tell everyone," Tami said. "Once you're empowered and educated about money, go and teach others. By doing that, no one will ever have to be a victim or feel helpless again. My daughter will never have to say, 'I can't do that,' whether it's going to Italy or contributing to the food bank. Having choices gives you power."

AS WE DRAW TO A CLOSE

Tami's story, regardless of her circumstances, is universal in its application. It speaks of the power and possibilities available to everyone. Let her, and all the others you met in these pages, be stirring examples of how profoundly life can change for you, too, when the Five Steps become a way of life.

Then, in the words of poet Maya Angelou, "As soon as healing takes place, go out and heal somebody else." If each of us would take those words to heart, imagine the difference we could make. Overcoming underearning gives you the power to not only transform your life, but to make a significant impact (by way of your example and your increased resources) on the lives of countless others. There's no doubt in my mind, the world will be so much better for it.

As the Fairy Godmother said to the farmer, I now say to you: "Believe me, this is only the beginning."

Conversation with Myself

(Note: This Conversation is different. Write your responses on a separate piece of paper, as a letter to yourself.)

How do you want your life to look in six months? How much do you want to be earning? What do you want to be doing? Where do you want to be living? Who do you want to be with?

Describe this scenario in as much detail as you wish, as if you're writing yourself a letter about what's already happened. Then put this letter in an envelope, address it to yourself, and attach a stamp. *Important—do not mail it yourself.* Give the envelope to a trusted friend, and ask him or her to mail it to you in six months.

TALK TO ME!

I'd love to hear your reactions when you read your letter in six months. In fact, I'd love to hear about any success you've achieved, or words of wisdom you'd like to pass along. Please visit my Web site, www.BarbaraStanny .com, and share your experiences. Your story may be the very one that inspires someone else to change.

> "Your task, to build a better world," God said. I answered, "How? This world is such a large, vast place, and there's nothing I can do."
>
> But God in all His wisdom said, "Just build a better you."
>
> —*Source unknown*

Appendix

Glossary

Affirmations—Positive statements used to program your subconscious.
Authentic Voice—The part of you who wants to become more of who you are, live the life you were meant to live, and make a difference in the world.

Big Lie—Untruths you've been telling yourself about yourself.
Bitch—Babe in Total Control of Herself.
Blanche—The critical or disapproving voices in your head.

The Click—That "aha" moment when you recognize, with every fiber of your being, that you deserve to earn more for no other reason than you're worth it.
Codependence—A psychological condition in which you ignore your own needs and desires to concentrate on, control, or caretake others.
Confidantes—Those you can talk to about your attitudes toward money and your efforts to change.

Dawdlers—Workshop graduates who didn't make many changes.
Decision versus Goal—A goal denotes the desired destination; a decision implies the determination to reach it.
Defining Truth—The realization that no one is doing this to you. You are doing it to yourself. Therefore, you have the ability to change it.
Deprivation—A condition in which your emotional and/or physical needs are not being met; not only a deficiency of money, but time, freedom, choices, joy, power, and a sense of your own value.
Discomfort Zone—The space between where you are now and where you want to be.
Doers—Workshop graduates who made significant changes.
Doers Who Didn't—Workshop graduates who made huge strides in all sorts of ways . . . *except* in their earnings.

Financial Independence—Having the resources to live a satisfying, comfortable life, accomplish your dreams and goals, and have more fun doing what you do.

First Law of Investing—Never put money in anything you don't understand, whether it's a stock, a bond, or the market itself.

Grand Conundrum—A deeply embedded, rarely conscious internal conflict, often between the comfort motive and the profit motive.

Inner Work—Transforming your thoughts, feelings, beliefs, attitudes, and decisions about yourself and money; personal awareness.

Messengers—Those who have a referral, an idea, a job lead, or some communication that provides forward momentum.

Mindful low earner—One who holds a low-paying job because it feeds his or her soul and still offers adequate income.

Outer Work—The mechanics of marketing yourself, negotiating higher pay, and managing your money; practical strategies.

Overcoming Underearning Promise—Small steps consistently taken lead to remarkable results.

Profit Motive—A firm decision to make more money.

Recommended Game Plan for Overcoming Underearning—Think big. Act small. And never, ever stop until you attain your goal, no matter what.

Self-esteem—Seeing yourself as having value.

Selfish—What you are when you're not doing what someone else wants you to do.

Stretch—Doing what you think you can't do.

True Believers—Those who recognize your potential, offer you encouragement, and celebrate even your tiniest success.

Underearner—One who earns less than her potential despite her need or desire to do otherwise; a condition of low self-esteem.

Underearner Whine—"This is soooo hard." (The truth: overcoming underearning is not hard, but it *is* uncomfortable.)

Voluntary Simplicity—A conscious choice to live on less in order to create a simpler, saner life.

Way Showers—Role models who provide you with a map or serve as proof that success is possible.

Wealth Builder—Someone who makes sure her money works as hard for her as she does for it.

Recommended Resources

There are so many great resources available, I could never mention them all. Instead, I've listed a few of my favorites and those recommended by my interviewees. Consider these a starting point.

For more options, and the very latest Web addresses, check my Web site: www.barbarastanny.com. It's loaded with all kinds of free resources, tips, articles, quotes, and affirmations.

I'd really love to hear what Web sites, books, publications, or other materials you've found especially helpful. Please contact me through my Web site.

FINANCIAL EDUCATION

These sites are just the tip of a very vast iceberg.

www.choosetosave.org/tools. This site has over a hundred calculators for every possible financial question.

www.npfe.org. The National Partners for Financial Empowerment is a coalition of organizations devoted to improving personal financial skills.

www.aaii.com. The nonprofit American Association of Individual Investors provides some of the best financial education seminars I've attended.

A few other sites I like: www.smartmoney.com, www.forbes.com, www.fool.com, and www.kiplingers.com.

SALARY AND NEGOTIATION

Here are my recommendations for the latest salary figures, job leads, and articles about negotiation.
www.monster.com
www.jobweb.com
www.salary.com

STARTING A BUSINESS

www.sba.gov. The Small Business Administration has an easy-to-navigate site filled with everything you need to know about going into business for yourself.

www.startupjournal.com. The *Wall Street Journal*'s online center for entrepreneurship.

www.count-me-in.org. Founded by Nell Merino, who started Take Your Daughter to Work Day, this site is all about helping women get financing for their businesses.

GETTING OUT OF DEBT

www.debtorsanonymous.org. I highly recommend this twelve-step organization to anyone struggling with financial problems. It also offers free literature, including a pamphlet on underearning.

www.financialrecovery.com. The Financial Recovery Institute provides cutting-edge resources and coaching. The Money Minder Express is by far the best tool I've seen for tracking expenses and creating a spending plan.

www.annualcreditreport.com. Log on here to order a free annual credit report. You can also call 1-877-322-8228.

FINANCIAL PLANNING

www.cfp.net; www.napfa.com. Tells you how to find an advisor, check out his or her history, the right questions to ask, along with personal finance tools.

www.wiseradvisor.com. An independent and unbiased matching service designed to help individuals find the best financial advisors for their needs.

www.planning.yahoo.com. Lots of articles and resources for finding and working with advisors.

ESPECIALLY FOR WOMEN (MEN WELCOMED, TOO!)

www.wife.org. The Women's Institute for Financial Education (tag line: "Every woman needs a wife!") was started by two financial professionals. It's chock-full of financial information and issues related to women. Check out the money clubs. They're fabulous!

www.bluesuitmom.com. If you're a working mom, you'll love this site.

www.msmoney.com. One of the first women's financial sites. It survived the dot-com bust and has improved with age.

www.womenswallstreet.com. A major portal site for women and money.

www.wiseupwomen.org. Brought to you by the Department of Labor Women's Bureau. Try their free teleclasses.

www.ivillage.com. A virtual wealth of financial information is available under the Home and Parenting sections.

PUBLICATIONS

Wall Street Journal. Even if you don't subscribe, I urge you to read Jonathan Clement's column in Wednesday's *Journal* (Section D on personal finance).

Money magazine, *Smart Money Magazine*, *Business Week*. In my opinion, they are the best, most comprehensive financial magazines around.

New York Times. A valuable resource, especially the Sunday "Business" section. It's worth a subscription!

BOOKS

My All-Time Favorites
The Richest Man in Babylon, by George S. Clason (Plume, 1926). If you read no other finance book, this will tell you everything you need to know to become a Wealth Builder.

Money Is My Friend, by Phil Laut (Trinity Publications, 1978). A splendid in-depth look at how crucial the Inner Work is to creating wealth. It's filled with fabulous exercises.

Personal Finance for Dummies, by Eric Tyson (IDG Books, 1994). I really like all the "Dummies" books about money, but this just happens to be my favorite.

Rich Dad, Poor Dad, by Robert Kiyosaki (Warner Books, 2000). A highly entertaining parable that's a powerhouse of a book. I was surprised how many people I interviewed mentioned this title and how it motivated them.

Books Particularly Relevant to Overcoming Underearning
Start Late, Finish Rich, by David Bach (Broadway Books, 2005). I love all of David's books. He's a prolific and engaging writer, offering solid advice. This one, however, has the most extensive section on earnings.

Nice Girls Don't Get Rich (Warner, 2005) and *Nice Girls Don't Get the Corner Office* (Warner, 2004), by Lois Frankel. Every aspiring high earner (including men) should read both these books. Down-to-earth guidance in very short chapters, a pithy guide to everything you need to know to get ahead and stay ahead.

Why Women Earn Less, by Mikelann Valterra (Career Press, 2004), and *Why Men Earn More,* by Warren Farrell (AMACOM, 2005). I thought these make a nice matched set. Each is very interesting, with very differing slants.

Inspirational Books

The Four Agreements, by Don Miguel Ruiz (Amber-Allen, 1997). Simple, practical, gorgeously written primer for achieving personal freedom and power.

Excuse Me, Your Life is Waiting, by Lynn Grabhorn (Hampton Roads, 2003). A simple plan for shifting your thinking and profoundly changing your life through the power of your emotions.

Codependent No More, by Melody Beattie (Hazelton, 1992). One of the first—and in my opinion, still the best—primers for people stuck in the codependent pattern.

Negotiation Books

Getting to Yes: Negotiating Agreement without Giving In, by Roger Fisher (Penguin Books, 1981). This enduring classic is based on a Harvard research study.

Women Don't Ask: Negotiation and Gender Divide, by Linda Babcock (Princeton University Press, 2003). I want every working woman to read this book, which is also based on extensive research.

Negotiation for Dummies, by Michael Donaldson (IDG, 1996). You just can't make negotiation any simpler than this, and it's excellent material.

Ways to Trim Your Spending

by Marcia Brixey
Founder of Money Wi$e Women
www.moneywisewomen.net

In order to get more money for something you really want, you need to spend less money on something else.

- Before you buy something, ask yourself five questions: Do I really want this? Do I need this? Will I use this? Am I buying this because it's on sale? Do I really love this?
- Before using your credit card to purchase, ask yourself if the item will be usable after you finish making payments.
- Ask yourself, "Would I buy this item if I were paying cash?"
- Before purchasing, ask yourself, "Is this item important for my future?"
- Before purchasing, ask yourself, "How long will this be useful to me?"
- Keep an "I WANT LIST."
- Set money limits before you go shopping.
- Resolve to cut one expense that doesn't bring you joy or prosperity.
- Lock your credit card up in your safe-deposit box—don't use it!!
- Never carry a credit card unless you plan to use it.
- Avoid paying costly ATM fees by using the ATM at your bank.
- Never shop for recreation. Plan your purchases.
- Before you buy anything that costs more than $100, wait twenty-four hours.
- Shop at local resale shops, discount centers, and factory outlets.
- Buy generic items in the grocery store.
- Plan menus before you go grocery shopping.
- Shop with a list and stick to it!
- Don't make any impulse purchases.
- Don't overbuy just because it's on sale.

- Don't buy any new clothes until you have your present wardrobe paid for.
- Think twice before buying clothing that requires dry cleaning.
- Own an economy car—preferably a used economy car.
- Maintain your car properly so it will last longer.
- Learn how to change your own oil. Changing the oil every three thousand to five thousand miles can save hundreds of dollars a year and preserve the life of your car.
- Never pass up a garage sale, but only buy what you need or are looking for.
- Stop subscribing to magazines you don't read.
- Vacation at off-season rates.
- Save your spare change every day. Put it in a jar and open a savings account at the end of the month.
- If you get a raise, cost of living increase, or unexpected cash, save it—don't spend it.
- Take your lunch to work. Treat yourself to eat lunch out one to two times a month.
- Skip the daily latte and bring your coffee to work.
- Cut your cable television to basic.
- Don't buy videos—rent them instead.
- Go to matinee movies instead of the more expensive regular hour movies.
- Use long-distance calling cards—many of them are much less expensive.
- Make hair appointments every six weeks instead of every four weeks.
- Do your own manicures or share with a friend.
- Color your own hair.
- Watch for free events in your area.
- Stay clear of fast-food restaurants.
- Always turn off electrical appliances that are not being used.
- Run the dishwasher and washing machine only with full loads.
- Keep your thermostat at sixty-eight degrees during the winter. Turn your heat off at night.
- Plan errands carefully to cover the least amount of mileage.
- Examine your car insurance and home insurance deductibles. If you raise your deductibles, you will reduce your premiums.
- Reduce your mortgage payments by refinancing.
- If you carry mortgage insurance (PMI), make sure you really need it or ask your lender to drop it.
- After a loan is repaid, make the payments to yourself instead of the bank.

Hiring a Financial Advisor

The best way to find a financial advisor is by asking everyone you know for names. But don't make the four biggest mistakes people make when hiring an advisor.

1. Interviewing only one advisor. Never make a decision until you've talked with *at least three*. (The interview process is an education in itself!)
2. *Not checking the advisor's history.* Ask the advisor for a copy of SEC Form ADV, which discloses any prior complaints (required by law). Also contact www.nasd.com (National Association of Security Dealers; 1-888-846-2722) and www.sec.gov (Securities and Exchange Commission; 1-800-732-0330) for background checks.
3. Failing to think through this question: *What do I want from an advisor?*
4. Neglecting to ask the advisor enough questions. *There's no such thing as a dumb question.* Just make sure you understand the answers. If not, keep asking until you do. After all, you're hiring them; they're working for you.

QUESTIONS TO ASK A FINANCIAL ADVISOR

Here's a basic list. Add anything else you want to know.

1. What experience do you have? Education? Qualifications? Credentials?
2. How long have you been in the business?
3. What services do you offer?
4. What is your approach to financial planning? How would you describe your investment style?
5. Will you be the only person working with me? How often do you meet with clients?

6. How are you paid for your services? Fees, commission, or a combination of both?
7. How much do you typically charge?
8. Have you ever been disciplined for unlawful or unethical actions?
9. Will you give me the name of other clients I can talk to, especially those in circumstances similar to mine?
10. Is there anything else I should know that I haven't asked?

Affirmations

Affirmations are positive statements expressed as if they've already happened.

Choose one or two of these affirmations to work with, or create your own.
Write them on note cards and post where you'll see them.
Read them out loud several times a day.

I am confident in my ability to make money.

I always live below my means.

I love money and appreciate what it does for me.

I am very optimistic about my financial future.

I value what I do and who I am.

I am secure around money.

I am paid what I am worth.

I am passionate about my work.

I have supportive nurturing relationships.

I like wealthy people.

I am debt free.

I rise to situations which are beyond my abilities.

I am resilient and able to bounce back.

I am filled with gratitude for the success I've achieved.

I am delighted to delegate and set limits.

I am tenacious in achieving my goals.

I am attracting the perfect people to help me reach my goals.

Others:

Index